JOE PENHALL

# **Blue / Orange**

*with commentary and notes by*
RACHEL CLEMENTS

METHUEN DRAMA

**Bloomsbury Methuen Drama**
An imprint of Bloomsbury Publishing Plc

50 Bedford Square          175 Fifth Avenue
London                     New York
WC1B 3DP                   NY 10010
UK                         USA

**www.bloomsbury.com**

*Blue/Orange* first published in Great Britain in 2000 by Methuen Drama
Revised edition published 2001

BRITISH LIBRARY CATALOGUING-IN-PUBLICATION DATA
A catalogue record for this book is available from the British Library.

ISBN: PB:     978-1-4081-4091-8

LIBRARY OF CONGRESS CATALOGING-IN-PUBLICATION DATA
A catalogue record for this book is available from the Library of Congress.

Typeset by Country Setting, Kingsdown, Kent CT14 8ES
Printed and bound in Great Britain

# Contents

# Joe Penhall

1993    *Wild Turkey* (one-act play) premiered at the London
        New Play Festival, Old Red Lion, directed by Keith
        Mattock.
1994    *Some Voices* premiered at the Royal Court Theatre,
        London, directed by Ian Rickson.
1995    One year writer-in-residency at the National Theatre.
        *Pale Horse* premiered at the Royal Court, directed by
        Ian Rickson.
        *Some Voices* wins the John Whiting Award.
        *Pale Horse* wins the Thames Television (Pearson's)
        Award.
1997    *Love and Understanding* premiered at the Bush Theatre,
        London, directed by Mike Bradwell.
        Appointed Literary Associate at the Donmar Warehouse,
        London.
1998    *Love and Understanding* first produced in the US at Long
        Wharf, Connecticut, directed by Mike Bradwell.
        *The Bullet* premiered at the Donmar Warehouse,
        directed by Dominic Cooke.
2000    *Blue/Orange* premiered at the Cottesloe, National
        Theatre, directed by Roger Michell, winning the *Evening
        Standard* Best Play Award and the Critics' Circle Award
        for Best New Play.
        Screenplay *Some Voices* produced for FilmFour.
2001    *Blue/Orange* transferred to the Duchess Theatre in the
        West End and wins the Olivier Award for Best New Play.
2004    *Dumb Show* premiered at the Royal Court Theatre
        Jerwood Theatre Downstairs.
        Screenplay *Enduring Love* (adapted from the novel by Ian
        McEwan) produced for FilmFour.
        *The Long Firm*, a four-part serial, produced for the BBC,
        and BAFTA-nominated for Best Serial.

# Plot

*Act One*

The play opens in a hospital consultation room at the start of a conversation between Bruce (a junior doctor) and Christopher (his patient). In the room, there is a water cooler and a bowl of oranges. The two men seem to have a reasonably good rapport, although there appears to be some tension around the fact that it is Christopher's 'big day'. Christopher is fidgety and agitated, and the two men have a conversation about the kinds of drinks that Christopher should be avoiding (such as coffee, Coke and alcohol). As the conversation turns to drugs, Bruce seems to be slightly losing control of the consultation, but tries to get his patient to discuss why he is in hospital. We learn that Christopher has been diagnosed with borderline personality disorder.

Just as Bruce is starting to explain to Christopher how he believes that 'recent developments' might warrant a reconsideration of this diagnosis, Robert enters with a cup of coffee. Without addressing Christopher at all, Robert launches into a conversation about his weekend and an evening spent with Bruce and his wife. Eventually, Bruce introduces Robert to Christopher as Dr Smith, a senior consultant, and explains that he's asked Robert to sit in on their session. Christopher seems put at once on edge both by Robert's presence and the fact that he has a cup of coffee and cigarettes. There is a small battle of wills between the three men, resulting in Christopher getting a number of cigarettes but Bruce drinking Robert's coffee. Christopher points out that when he leaves the hospital in twenty-four hours' time, he will be able to do what he likes, and we learn that he's already packed his bags to go. The consultation continues in a rather disrupted manner as Christopher gets increasingly agitated, leading to Bruce telling him that, outside the hospital, people would consider his behaviour to be that of – and here, he quotes Christopher – 'an "uppity nigger"'.

Bruce and Robert begin discussing Christopher's condition, and ask him to wait in another room for a few minutes. Christopher exits, telling the doctors that he hopes they aren't changing their minds about letting him go home because his 'twenty-eight days [are] up'. Bruce tells Robert that he wants to re-section Christopher (currently being held under Section 2 of the Mental Health Act 1983) because he believes that his diagnosis might be incorrect and that he may in fact be schizophrenic. Robert brushes this off, citing medical guidelines, 'ethics', and a lack of bed space, and even goes so far as to imply that Bruce should follow his advice if he doesn't want to jeopardise his career. The two doctors continue to disagree, voicing a range of arguments about the suitability of different kinds of psychiatric care, and are at variance over definitions of conditions and Christopher's diagnosis.

The conversation reaches an impasse, but Robert invites Christopher back into the room. Although Robert wants the assessment to be over, Bruce asks him to stay and listen to Christopher answering a few more questions. Bruce asks the patient what he sees in the fruit bowl. Christopher says that the oranges are bright blue. He also says, slightly reluctantly, that his father was the former dictator of Uganda, Idi Amin. Bruce asks Christopher to go back to his ward. Christopher senses that something has gone wrong, seeking reassurance that he is still going home.

Once their patient has left, Bruce and Robert continue to argue over their differing interpretations of Christopher's behaviour and beliefs. Bruce sees them as evidence of hallucination and delusion; Robert interprets them as neurotic behaviour which might be rooted in Christopher's upbringing. At this point, Robert begins to see Christopher as a potential case study for his own research on cultural specificity and mental health. As the argument continues to escalate, Robert pulls rank, pointing out that he has seniority and that what he says goes. Eventually, he agrees to conduct his own assessment of Christopher, claiming (despite earlier threats and insinuations) that he is on Bruce's side, and that they can make a decision about Christopher the next morning.

*Act Two*

Act Two takes place later the same night. It opens midway through a conversation between Robert and Christopher. The implication is that Christopher has voiced suicidal thoughts. However, Robert's response is an almost entirely self-centred monologue in which he discusses his own anxieties and professional jealousies, muses on the human condition, and tells Christopher to calm down because he is not actually suicidal. Christopher is incredulous about Robert's advice, and now starts to sound unsure about whether he actually wants to leave hospital. He describes being – or perhaps *feeling* like he's being – stared at, and describes hearing strange noises outside his flat. He also describes his loneliness and the fact that he doesn't have friends or a girlfriend. As in Act One, he says that he wants to go to Africa.

Robert tries to find out more about Christopher's upbringing, following up his earlier thoughts on Christopher's delusions. Christopher claims that he can 'prove' that he is Idi Amin's son, producing a newspaper article which he says his mother gave him, and which discusses Amin's wives, including one who supposedly lives in Feltham. Christopher continues to describe the problems with the area where he lives, but it's not clear whether he's describing real people or delusions.

When Christopher again says that he doesn't want to leave the hospital, Robert suggests that Bruce has manipulated Christopher's thoughts and feelings, which further distresses and confuses Christopher. Robert tells Christopher that if he leaves hospital, he will take his case over from Bruce, and it becomes clear that he is indeed hoping to use Christopher as a case study for his research. Christopher becomes increasingly adamant that he agrees with Bruce that he's not ready to go home, and goes so far as to say that he was lying when he said, in Act One, that he wanted to leave. Robert claims that he understands the health system and its prejudices better than Bruce, and tries to explain his theories of cultural specificity and institutional racism. Christopher becomes extremely agitated, thinking that Bruce has sectioned him because he is black. As Robert attempts to calm him down, Christopher

tells Robert about the conversation that he and Bruce had
about recreational drugs, claiming that Bruce told him
that recreational drugs are more fun than medical ones,
and that Bruce has been lying to him.

*Act Three*
Act Three takes place the next afternoon. Bruce and
Christopher are in the consultation room and Bruce is reading
aloud from a report that has been sent to the hospital
authority. The report complains of Bruce's conduct with
Christopher, accusing him of being 'provocative, unconventional,
patronising' and of 'using the racial epithet, nigger'. Bruce is
flabbergasted and asks Christopher whether he really believes
the charges of the report. Christopher now says that he doesn't
know, but that he just wants to go home.

  Robert enters, and reveals that the report was presented at
a management hearing that morning, but Robert claims that
he knows about it because he is 'on' the Authority. Bruce asks
Christopher to go back to his ward, and Christopher again
voices concerns that the doctors might be about to try to
detain him against his will. Once Christopher has left, Bruce
asks Robert whether he knows what the report says. Robert
claims to have read the report, but as Bruce reads further
extracts out, it becomes clear that Robert is the report's author.
Bruce wants the report to be withdrawn, but Robert says that
a procedure has now been set in motion and Bruce needs to
give his own statement of events.

  Bruce works out that the report suggests that Christopher
should be transferred to Robert's care and, though Robert
claims expediency and Christopher's interests as the reasons
behind this, Bruce suggests that this is an attempt for Robert to
further his own research. As Bruce becomes more irate and
more insulting to his colleague, Robert begins to question
Bruce's own mental health, and Bruce tears up the report.
Robert calls Reception to ask Christopher to come back, but
when Bruce tells Robert that he wants to speak to Christopher
alone, Robert claims this is not possible. Further, he reveals
that he's been keeping a diary in which he records Bruce's

behaviour and which he intends to show to the hospital's management. He claims that Bruce has been consistently insubordinate, racist, and obstructive to his research. Bruce explodes, challenging Robert's interpretation of his behaviour and also claiming that Robert's research is a waste of time and money.

Christopher arrives with his belongings. Robert tells him that he can leave after Bruce has asked him a few more questions. However, when Bruce tries to ask Christopher whether he was upset by any of Bruce's behaviour, Robert intervenes, saying that as Bruce is under investigation pending suspension from his post, he can't ask Christopher such questions. The doctors argue at some length about Christopher's diagnosis and the likely outcomes of him either leaving or remaining in hospital. The argument becomes personal, and Robert suggests that Bruce needs to contact a lawyer.

Bruce turns back to Christopher, passing him another orange, and asks whether Christopher was upset by Bruce's behaviour the previous day. Despite Robert's protestations, Christopher says that he was interested, not upset. Bruce asks him what colour the orange was, and, when Christopher says it was blue, Bruce asks him to peel the orange he is currently holding to see what colour it is. Again, Christopher says it is blue, and Bruce asks what Christopher thinks this means. Christopher says it relates to his father and gets the newspaper article out, but Bruce tells him to put it away. Bruce tells Robert that he thinks Christopher cut the article out of a newspaper. Robert continues to believe that Christopher's mother gave it to him until Bruce reveals that, that morning, Christopher has claimed that his father was Muhammad Ali.

It becomes clear that the complaint to the hospital authority was lodged by Robert. Christopher becomes more and more agitated, and Bruce now insists that he must speak to Christopher alone. Reluctantly, Robert leaves. Bruce tries to explain the severity of the situation, for both of them. He asks Christopher not to go ahead with the complaint and tries to explain why he believes Christopher may have been incorrectly diagnosed. When Christopher isn't very receptive to this,

Bruce becomes extremely agitated, calling him 'an idiot'.
Christopher (following Robert's earlier advice) starts laughing,
and, not realising that Robert has come back, Bruce loses his
temper completely. Robert overhears Bruce being verbally
abusive to Christopher – he only stops when he realises Robert
is there. Robert discharges Christopher from the hospital.
Before he leaves, Christopher asks the doctors, of the orange,
'Have you ever stuck your dick in one of these?', saying that he
once tried it with a grapefruit. We assume that this is probably
what led to him being sectioned in the first place.

   After Christopher has left, Bruce attempts to rescue the
situation, trying to apologise and make amends. However,
Robert tells him that, as far as he is concerned, Bruce's job in
the hospital is over. The play ends with Bruce asking to lodge
his own complaint with the hospital authority: he is ready to
make his statement.

# Commentary

Writing his column rounding up the year's theatre, published in the *Sunday Times* on 31 December 2000, John Peter opened by saying that:

> The big event of my year was what it should always be: a new play. Joe Penhall's *Blue/Orange* exploded in the National's Cottesloe like a thunderclap: an angry and fiercely compassionate play about those in the medical profession who put rank and power before healing.

There are a number of reasons for considering Joe Penhall's *Blue/Orange* to be a vital piece of work. It is an exceptionally well-crafted play, which has won a host of awards, and has produced some star performances from a number of well-known actors. It is, as Sarah Hemming said in a 'Platform Interview' with Penhall at the National Theatre in June 2000, 'sharp, fast, funny, argumentative, ambiguous'. More importantly, though, it has considerable significance as a contemporary example of what we might call an 'issue-conscious' play, its themes and concerns resonating potently with a wider set of political and social debates. As a play about race in the year of the Macpherson Report (into police behaviour following the Stephen Lawrence murder), it comments on and contributes towards a dialogue around understanding racism and, in particular, institutional racism. As a play about mental health, it explores a range of tensions around the diagnosis and treatment of serious mental illness. And, perhaps most importantly, the play is interested in language as an instrument of power, and the way it can be abused and 'spun' in the pursuit of institutional agendas. As we will see, this amounts to a critique of the New Labour culture of spin. In short, *Blue/Orange* works beyond the immediate scope of its own plot, characters and themes, engaging with a number of important political debates, social concerns and philosophical issues that have shaped and influenced contemporary British society.

## Context and Background

*Penhall, British theatre and representations of madness*

> Occasionally I've upset people with so-called outspokenness. People don't like a loudmouth. And I don't understand it. It's part of my job to be a thorn in the flesh. It comes naturally to me.
>
> Joe Penhall, interview with Jasper Rees,
> *Daily Telegraph*, 30 April 2001

Joe Penhall's first play, *Some Voices*, was first performed at London's Royal Court Theatre in 1994. John Peter, reviewing the play for the *Sunday Times*, called it 'the most thrilling playwriting debut in years'. As Aleks Sierz wrote in his influential book *In-Yer-Face Theatre: British Drama Today*, the production marked the start of 'a momentous era in the Court's history' (p. 210), as it opened a season of work by new young writers who also included Nick Grosso, Judy Upton and, most famously, Sarah Kane, whose first play *Blasted* premiered there at the start of 1995. Partly as a direct consequence of Penhall's inclusion in Sierz's book, the playwright is often considered alongside a range of other so-called 'in-yer-face' dramatists of the mid-1990s.

The mid-1990s saw a sudden explosion of British new writing for theatre, which was characterised, according to Sierz, by a particularly contemporary sensibility, a noticeably urban language loaded with sex, drugs, profanities, shocking acts of violence and a desire to shake the audience by the scruff of the neck. Including Kane's *Blasted*, Ravenhill's *Shopping and Fucking*, and works by Anthony Nielson, Patrick Marber, Philip Ridley and Jez Butterworth, and often focused on two of the powerhouses of British new writing, the Royal Court and the Bush Theatre, this sudden proliferation of exciting new works which spoke to a range of current issues and young audiences marked an important development in British theatre.

However, it would be a mistake to position Penhall too squarely among this group of writers (indeed, since none of these playwrights ever considered themselves part of a clearly defined 'movement', the same might go for any of them). In Penhall's case though, as Sierz himself notes, there are a number of factors which mean that understanding his work requires a broader context. With the exception of his first two, his plays do not tend towards physical violence (although, as we will see, other kinds of violence can be just as damaging). Penhall's writing is also much more nuanced than that of many in-yer-face writers, and reflects his awareness of the history of political writing in post-war British theatre. Playwrights of the 1960s through the 1980s such as Trevor Griffiths, David Edgar and Peter Nichols form part of a tradition which clearly informs Penhall's ideas of character, structure, narrative, metaphor, and dialectical debate, as we will explore in more detail later in this commentary.

Despite the fact that Penhall's work is very explicitly set in contemporary Britain (more specifically, in London), it would also be a mistake to focus too narrowly on the British tradition, particularly when considering *Blue/Orange* and Penhall's first piece, *Some Voices*. Both plays explore the terrain of mental health and, in particular, of schizophrenia. The social and medical contexts which inform them will be discussed in the following section, but it is worth paying some attention to the literary traditions around the representation of madness. Penhall is not, of course, the first writer to think about and explore ideas about madness: this has been an issue of concern over a wide range of periods, places and contexts. Indeed, there is a considerable body of criticism which (often indebted to Michel Foucault's seminal text *Madness and Civilization*) analyses the way that representations of madness at different points illuminate a whole range of issues pertaining to the contemporary ideas about health, of difference, of mortality and of social relations. From Hamlet's feigned madness, to the way in which the Duchess of Malfi is tormented by being surrounded by a spectacle of madmen, to the despair of Büchner's Woyzeck, there have been numerous theatrical representations of madness.

In Penhall's case, though, the most useful context for the representation of madness in *Blue/Orange* (and *Some Voices*) is the post-war period. In American literature of the 1950s and 1960s there was a strong tradition of exploring the idea of madness as a way into questioning and challenging accepted notions of so-called 'normal' society. A whole range of countercultural writers, including Allen Ginsberg (who is mentioned in *Blue/Orange*), Jack Kerouac, William Burroughs in *Naked Lunch* (1959), Ken Kesey in *One Flew Over the Cuckoo's Nest* (1962) and Charles Bukowski explore the figure of the outsider who challenges the 'madness' of power structures in society and is in turn constructed as 'mad'. Penhall has also mentioned being influenced by the short stories of Raymond Carver, vignettes which are frequently peopled by characters whose often rather mundane lives are in a state of dismal chaos.

But if Penhall was influenced by these writers, his plays are also clearly distinguished from some of their ideas and sensibilities. In *Some Voices*, which focuses on Ray, who suffers from schizophrenia and has just been released from hospital into 'care in the community' (in the form of his estranged, if well-intentioned, brother, Pete), Sierz states that 'Penhall sees parallels between schizophrenia and the "human condition"' (*In-Yer-Face Theatre*, p. 211). He quotes the writer as saying that, 'Anyone who is living in a big city, as Ray is, knows that it can drive you insane' (pp. 211–12), and suggests that, for Penhall, schizophrenia is 'a potent symbol of urban alienation' (p. 214). This is a reasonable point, but Penhall's work is very definitely 'not making the facile point that the "mad" are sane and the "sane" are mad' (John Peter, *Sunday Times*). Indeed, when some reviewers of *Blue/Orange* claimed that one of the play's strengths is that we never know how unwell Christopher actually is, Penhall's response was unequivocal. In an interview with Jasper Rees for the *Daily Telegraph*, he said: 'There were a lot of people fluttering around going, "What's so fascinating is that he might not be [schizophrenic]." That's liberal wishful thinking: he really is sick.' And in an interview with Hildegard Klein he pointed out that 'the idea that the mad are sane and the sane are mad is a cliché' (Mireia Aragay *et al.*, *British*

*Theatre of the 1990s*, p. 85). We will return to the issues around the representation of Christopher's illness and the way in which it structures the play, but here it's worth noting that, although we can position Penhall's work in relation to earlier countercultural explorations, it should not be seen as an entirely straightforward continuation of their ideas.

The connections between *Some Voices* and *Blue/Orange* are readily apparent: Penhall's return to the subject matter of mental health led to him being, for a while, regarded as – in his words to Sarah Hemming – the 'spokesperson of craziness', though he claimed this was unintentional. Both plays take some of their inspiration from Penhall's personal experience of having friends with the illness, briefly working in a centre for those with schizophrenia while in the United States, and from his experience as a local journalist in London during the early 1990s. There are, of course, key differences between the plays, most significantly in their setting and focus. In *Some Voices*, the play follows Ray, and looks at the failures of the 'care in the community' system from the perspective of the care user and the family: we never see any health professionals. *Blue/Orange*, of course, focuses on two doctors and institutional issues and implications rather than Christopher's experience or illness.

In this regard, the play bears comparison with some of Penhall's other works. In *Pale Horse*, first performed at the Royal Court in 1995, Penhall looks at the strange terrain of grief, and the play includes scenes with an undertaker, a vicar and a GP who all seem woefully ill-equipped for dealing with the emotional turmoil which we assume they must be faced with on a daily basis. In *Love and Understanding* (Bush Theatre, 1997), two of the characters are young doctors struggling with their responsibilities and relationship, but the play's real point of interest is the character of Richie, a freelance journalist who returns from overseas to stay on Neal and Rachel's sofa and further complicate their dissatisfaction. Like *Blue/Orange*, the play is a three-hander, and it is here that we see Penhall's interest in 'communication and manipulation' start to develop: as he said to Klein, 'Because Richie is witty, we like him, they like him. I think that's a very political thing' (p. 82).

Penhall's next play, *The Bullet* (Donmar Warehouse, 1998)
looks at the corrosive effects of redundancy, while the play that
followed *Blue / Orange*, *Dumb Show* (Royal Court, 2004), follows a
jaded comedian who becomes the subject of a tabloid sting.
Although the plots of *The Bullet* and *Dumb Show* have little
similarity to *Blue / Orange*, we can identify a shared concern
with the effects of institutions on individuals; and it also
becomes clear that, as Dominic Cavendish pointed out in his
*Daily Telegraph* review of *Landscape with Weapon* (National
Theatre, 2007), 'More than any of his peers, this former
journalist has shown a rare aptitude for confronting headline
issues of the day, using his gift of the gab as a dramatist to
interrogate their underlying complexities and contradictions.'
*Landscape with Weapon*, like *Blue / Orange* and *Haunted Child* (Royal
Court, 2011) is structured around 'a fraught dialogue between
a rampant idealist and a stoical pragmatist' (Aleks Sierz, *Tribune*,
23 December 2011). But where *Blue / Orange* is particularly
interesting in this regard is in the complexity with which this
debate is staged, so that it becomes difficult, at times, to know
which character is the idealist and which the pragmatist.

Penhall has also become increasingly well-known for his
work for television and film. Besides adapting both *Some Voices*
and *Blue / Orange* (the former into a film starring Daniel Craig
as Ray and David Morrissey as Pete; the latter into a TV film
which is discussed in the final section of this commentary), he
has worked on a number of major projects (the most famous of
which is his screenplay of Cormac McCarthy's *The Road*). His
adaptation of Ian McEwan's novel *Enduring Love* also has a
central motif of mental ill-health, while his adaptation of Jake
Arnott's *The Long Firm* into a TV mini-series is a character
study of a set of 1960s criminals, and is particularly concerned
with issues of corruption. His original work, the TV series
*Moses Jones*, which starred Shaun Parkes as a black detective,
ordered to investigate ritual killings and violence within
London's Ugandan community, simply because Jones is also
black, works with many of the issues around race, community
and belonging which are present in *Blue / Orange*, but in a very
different genre and to very different effect.

Although his most recent theatre works (*Love and Understanding,
Haunted Child*, and the 2012 play *Birthday*) focus on a distinctly
middle-class milieu, at the time of writing *Blue/Orange* Penhall
has described how he tended to write about characters who
were somehow disenfranchised, and had located much of his
impetus for writing at all in the fact that he was 'naturally
angry'. So what, in 2000, was there to be angry about?

*Social and political context: policy, psychiatry, race*
Penhall began work on the play that became *Blue/Orange* in
the mid-1990s, but wrote the piece as it stands today over the
course of a few weeks in 1999. Although the play was first
performed well into the third year of Tony Blair's tenure as
Prime Minister, and the play is distinctly marked by a concern
with some of New Labour's approaches, to make sense of the
political context of the piece, we need to look a little further
back, to the General Election of 1979.

*Thatcher and Blair*
In May 1979, Margaret Thatcher became Prime Minister of
Britain, leading a Conservative Party that swept to power to the
dismay of many on the political left. Thatcher's Conservatives
and their policies were markedly more right-wing than any
other post-war government, and were explicit in their aim to
roll back the Welfare State which previous governments,
following principles of liberalism and socialism, had sought to
sustain. Many of the agendas and policies which were central
to Thatcherism (as distinct from the Conservatism of the early
and mid-twentieth century) are still affecting Britain several
decades later. Most important is the 'Thatcherite' attitude to
the economy. The belief was that all areas of the economy
should be open to competition – that the market should be left
to its own devices rather than being subject to government
control and regulation. Thatcher began a programme of
privatisation, starting with the major industries and the rail
network. This policy went hand-in-hand with a shift in values
towards competition, individualism and individual choice,
whereby money became the main measure of success.

Perhaps the most infamous soundbite of Thatcher's tenure as Prime Minister is the phrase, which came from an interview with a women's magazine, 'there is no such thing as society'. In her memoir, Thatcher points out that her critics failed to look at what she said next – which is of particular resonance in relation to *Blue / Orange*:

> There are individual men and women, and there are families. And no government can do anything except through people, and people must look to themselves first. It's our duty to look after ourselves and then to look after our neighbour.
>
> Margaret Thatcher, *The Downing Street Years*
> (London: HarperCollins, 1993), p. 626

This attitude was indicative of the return to 'Victorian virtues' associated with Thatcherism, which centred on the traditional family, the value of hard work and resilience and the belief that everyone could succeed if they just put enough effort in; and it was key to the move towards 'care in the community', which I will discuss in the next section, and which forms the backdrop to Penhall's play.

In 1997, after thirteen years of Thatcher's premiership and another five with John Major leading another Conservative government, everything changed – or so many hoped. Tony Blair's victory with a modernised Labour Party rebranded as 'New' Labour was ushered in to the sounds of 'Things Can Only Get Better' and the sight of artists and musicians leading the celebrations. But – although there were, indeed, a number of key changes and developments – there was much continuity between the Thatcherite and Blairite years.

One of the major issues for the party, which quickly affected public perception, related to the increasing use of political 'spin'. In order to win the 1997 General Election, Blair and the architects of New Labour (whose main figures alongside Blair were Gordon Brown, Peter Mandelson and Alastair Campbell) had sought not just to rebrand the party but to carve out a new set of principles, known as the 'Third Way', which sought to position itself between the Old Left and the New Right, synthesising a sense of social justice and social democracy with a faith in the markets and acceptance of capitalist values. They also hoped to change the public perception of the Labour Party and to widen its appeal to voters by a changed media strategy, wooing the traditionally Tory-supporting papers including *The Sun*. According to Andrew Marr:

> On the way to winning power, New Labour turned itself into a kind of perpetual media newsdesk, with a plan for what every political headline should say every day, and an endless 'grid' of announcements, images, soundbites and rebuttals, constantly pressing down on journalists, their editors and owners, fighting for every adjective and exclamation mark.
>
> Marr, *A History of Modern Britain*
> (London: Macmillan, 2007), p. 568

In the long run, the strategy which won New Labour the election went on to do considerable damage both to Blair's government and to the public perception of politics in general. Over the course of a decade, public trust in politicians was severely eroded: where John Major's government, which was troubled by several sex and corruption scandals, gave new currency to the word 'sleaze', Blair's gave new currency to 'spin'. Gradually, everything that came from Number Ten's press office came to be distrusted. The situation reached a crisis point in 2003–04, a few years after Penhall's play, in a head-to-head between the government and the BBC over the accusation that Downing Street had 'sexed up' the intelligence dossier published in September 2002 which had been used to win over the public to support for the coming war in Iraq. But even before this now infamous set of events, which led to the death of Dr David Kelly (the probable source for journalist Andrew Gilligan's 'sexed up' quotation) and the Hutton Inquiry, there was a growing distrust of the ways in which information and ideas were being manipulated and represented by those in power. Although Penhall's play is set in a hospital, not in Parliament, it can be read directly in relation to this context.

*Mental health care and psychiatry*

In order to understand the issues around care and psychiatry in *Blue / Orange*, it is useful to know something not only about the political context of Britain in the year 2000, but about the longer history of schizophrenia and serious mental illness.

Before the twentieth century, there were few therapeutic options for those suffering from serious mental illness. In the first half of the century developments in psychiatry and psychoanalysis, motivated in part by the necessity for greater understanding following the First and Second World Wars, meant that more attention was given to mental health. However, in the UK and elsewhere, those with serious mental illnesses tended to be sedated and shut up in asylums. The establishment of the National Health Service in 1948 began a move towards greater equality of health care, and in the early 1950s the development of first-generation antipsychotic drugs effected a revolution in mental health care as, for the first time, some patients with chronic schizophrenia were able to receive treatment for some of the symptoms of their condition (for a brief outline of the illness, see the notes on p. 117). In 1957, after a century of steady increase, the numbers of patients in Britain's asylums started to drop relatively rapidly.

During the 1960s and 1970s the 'anti-psychiatry movement', which is associated with the work of the psychiatrists R. D. Laing and Thomas Szasz and the philosopher Michel Foucault, generated significant public interest. It's worth noting that these thinkers (and others, such as Franco Basaglia, Erving Goffman, David Cooper and Thomas Scheff) are by no means a homogenous group; their ideas and rationales vary consider-ably, and many of them either were or became uncomfortable with the 'anti-psychiatry' label – not least because a number were practising psychiatrists. However, there are key areas of similarity in terms of their concerns and intentions.

The anti-psychiatry movement challenged many of the basic principles and assumptions of psychiatry. It was principally concerned that definitions of psychiatric conditions are both arbitrary and vague, leaving much scope for (mis)interpretation, and argued that psychiatric practices were doing patients more harm than good. The anti-psychiatrists all believed that the terms and principles of psychiatry needed to be challenged, and the care of the mentally ill and society's attitudes to mental health to be revolutionised. Laing, for example, argued that mental illness was not so much a problem of the unwell individual but an issue generated by the family and by wider society. He was interested in developing understandings of psychosis, and, although he did not disagree with the fact that the mentally ill need treatment, he argued against a biological approach to mental health, placing emphasis on the role of society, culture and intellect in shaping an individual's experience. Szasz denounced the practices of the psychiatric institutions and doctors of his day, arguing that they were abusive and coercive. He was sceptical about the very notion of mental illness, and in 1960 published a book entitled *The Myth of Mental Illness*, arguing that psychiatry blurs the boundaries between disease and behaviour; in particular, he was strongly opposed to involuntary treatment.

Foucault, writing from a slightly different perspective – he was a philosopher, historian and social theorist rather than a psychiatrist – published one of the most influential histories of madness, *Madness and Civilization*, in 1961. In this work, Foucault looks at the ways in which madness has been treated, conceptualised and understood from the Middle Ages to the nineteenth century. Particularly noteworthy is Foucault's argument that the more recent approaches to madness (like the asylums of Europe in the nineteenth century) which seem at first sight humane, since they avoid physical restraint, are in practice just as controlling, their mechanisms relying less on external control than on patterns of judgement and punishment which are internalised by the patient. Foucault also raises questions about the relationship between the doctor and the patient and the generation of 'authority' which continue to be relevant to contemporary medicine, and which *Blue / Orange* also explores. His writing was instrumental in highlighting the ways in which, across time, the treatment of 'madness' has been involved in – and the unwell subject to – the operation of power and control.

Much of the work and many of the ideas of the anti-psychiatry movement are now treated as out of date. Developments in antipsychotic drugs, and the effectiveness of these at managing some conditions, mean that few would argue against medicating those with serious mental illnesses. Further, in the writings of many key voices in anti-psychiatry there is a tendency to romanticise mental illness: in response, we might think of Penhall's assertion that Christopher 'really is sick', or, the statement made at the end of *The Center Cannot Hold* (2007), a memoir written by Elyn Saks – who has schizophrenia and is also an extremely influential and successful professor of law in the USA – where she says that, were there a 'cure' for schizophrenia, she'd take it. But the work of the anti-psychiatry movement also developed many valuable ideas and arguments, particularly about the need to change systems of care and to listen to those with mental illnesses.

Meanwhile, in mainstream mental health, the declining numbers of patients in the asylums, the increasing availability of treatment options and the 1959 Mental Health Act (MHA) were gradually altering perceptions of mental health and making the notion of deinstitutionalisation a viable possibility. This was seen in the increase in outpatient numbers, the rise of day centres, and a move from asylums to district hospitals. Difficulties began to arise because, despite this movement of patients and care, funding was not reallocated or made available; and in 1959, according to Nicholas Timmins, the reality was that 'less had been spent per head on the mentally ill in the community than in 1951' (p. 28). In the 1980s, the government started closing and selling the old asylums, and moved towards the notion of 'care in the community', as the 1983 MHA emphasised patients' rights and the importance of community care. However, local authorities had few legal obligations to provide these services, and mental health was still stigmatised in practice and perceptions.

In 1986 came a damning report on the failed attempt to reshape community care, arguing, in Timmins's words, that 'the shift of resources to social services and the community side of the NHS needed to make community care a reality had simply not kept pace with the patient movement' and that 'the one option not tenable is to do nothing' (pp. 29–30). The move towards 'care in the community' – a policy brought about partly because of changing understandings and treatment, but also as a result of political expediency – was becoming 'a policy failure which was leaving the mentally ill on the streets' (Timmins, p. 30). Despite this, Thatcher's government continued to shrink the limits of state care, instead calling for familial responsibility (as stressed in her 'no such thing as society' statement) and individual effort. The Conservatives' market-led ideology further impacted on the 1990 Community Care Act which created an internal market within care systems. Under this piece of legislation, the state became an enabler, not a provider, of care. Although there have been improvements in care since the 1980s, and although New Labour had a number of key successes in relation to the NHS, in the late 1990s, Nick Bosanquet states clearly that 'for mental health there was still little access to low-cost non-drug interventions such as cognitive behavioural therapy' (Nick Bosanquet, 'The Health and Welfare Legacy' in *Blair's Britain*, p. 390).

Penhall's attitude to, and understanding of, the changes to the provision of mental health care under Thatcher is emphatic: as he said to Klein, '*Blue/Orange* is quite obviously about government legislation that hasn't worked' (p. 88). He, like many others, is deeply angered by the money-saving approach that led 'to slinging people out the first chance you get' on the faulty understanding that 'everyone can fend for themselves', pointing to levels of homelessness in the 1980s as a consequence of mental health legislation – and dramatised, in *Some Voices*, through the character of Ives who really does have nowhere to go on being released from hospital (Penhall's 'Platform Interview', 7 June 2000). *Blue/Orange* continues this critique.

*Multicultural Britain, the Macpherson Report and institutional racism*
If Penhall's willingness to broach sensitive issues such as mental health and schizophrenia made his play challenging, its voicing of concerns around institutional racism rendered it, in his words in the 'Platform Interview', 'right on the agenda'.

The impact of racism had been felt in Britain in insidious ways, having a marked impact on day-to-day life for many citizens throughout the post-war period. With the influx of legal immigrants from across the (rapidly shrinking) British Empire in the immediate post-war years (most famously, on the *Windrush*, which docked in the UK in June 1948, carrying 493 Jamaicans who wanted to start a new life in Britain, with footage of the ship sparking considerable unease and complaints from some MPs), through the 1960s and 1970s, British legislation became increasingly hostile to citizens from the colonies and, in particular, to non-white citizens, whose freedom to migrate became ever more limited. Thatcher continued this policy and approach through the 1980s.

More recently, debates about national identity and multiculturalism in a post-colonial era have proved complex and inflammatory, highlighting the fact that racism is a very real issue. Statistics on the police's 'stop-and-search' tactics also contribute to this picture: these measures caused considerable disquiet in the 1970s and 1980s, but figures have been kept on the searches only since 2005. In October 2007, the Ministry of Justice published figures which showed that black and Asian people are more likely to be stopped and searched than their white counterparts, particularly in London. (In 2005–06, black people were more than seven times more likely to be searched than whites.)

But the events which had the most lasting impact on Britain in terms of the understanding of race relations stemmed from the murder of Stephen Lawrence, a black eighteen-year-old man, who was killed by a group of five or six white men in a racist attack in south-east London in 1993. Following an incompetent police investigation, the Lawrence family brought a private prosecution which failed due to insufficient evidence. In 1997 the then Labour Home Secretary, Jack Straw, ordered an independent inquiry into the police investigation. Sir William Macpherson published his report, officially titled *The Inquiry into the Matters Arising from the Death of Stephen Lawrence*, in February 1999. Macpherson concluded that the initial police inquiry into Lawrence's murder was marred by errors and

incompetence; but most importantly he found that the
Metropolitan Police was 'institutionally racist'. This term had
been in usage since the Black Power movement in the USA in
the 1960s, but it was Macpherson's report which brought the
term – and, therefore, the issue – into the British public
consciousness. It was no longer possible to avoid the fact or
deny that racism was a current problem.

Following Macpherson's report and recommendations,
more institutions began self-investigating, and the theatre was
no exception. In June 2001, the Eclipse conference was held at
Nottingham Playhouse, its aims including discussing and
devising strategies to combat racism in theatre, and exploring
ways of developing our understanding and knowledge of
African Caribbean and Asian theatre. The findings of the
conference (its report was published in 2002) confirmed what
had long been known but unspoken: British theatre was
dominated – particularly in its upper levels of management
and artistic direction – by white people. The report quotes an
Arts Council of England survey from 1998 of nineteen arts
organisations which 'found that out of 2,900 staff, 177 (6%)
were either African Caribbean, Asian or Chinese, with 100 of
those staff working in the area of catering or Front of House.
One was employed at senior management level' (Eclipse
Report, p. 8). It made twenty-one recommendations for
combating institutional racism in arts institutions.

When *Blue / Orange* was first performed, then, it is clear from
the contextual material about Britain's politics, its mental
health care, and its developing understanding of its multiracial
society, that Penhall's play was cracking open a whole set of
issues of considerable concern. Talking to Klein, Penhall
posited the idea that theatre is a good art form for exploring
challenging issues, claiming that it is 'perhaps the best medium
because film tends to have more commercial concerns, in the
sense that it finds these subjects a little difficult to digest,
whereas the theatre loves them and eats them up' (p. 87).
However, he was wary of claiming too much efficacy for the
theatre, saying that:

As for trying to generate any kind of change, I don't know
that it does in the short term. In the long term, theatre, like
film, music and all the art forms, does have a very slow,
gradual effect on our society. [ . . . ] People see films of
theatre and hear music, and they do start to think about it,
and the status quo begins to change. It doesn't change the
whole society, only a very small minority that goes to the
theatre. But it does change those people and maybe, when
talking about it, they change other people.            (p. 87)

## Setting

*Blue/Orange* takes place in a single setting: a psychiatric hospital
in contemporary London. Penhall does not specify the set's
appearance in any more detail than this: '*A consultation room. A
transparent water cooler. A round table with a large glass bowl containing
three oranges*' (p. 5). While this leaves considerable room for
design interpretation, it is worth noting that the focus of the
text is really on the relationships between the characters.
Productions, and particularly the first at the National Theatre,
have tended to work with a minimal set. In his review for the
*Daily Mail* of Penhall's 2007 play, *Landscape with Weapon*, Patrick
Marmion wrote that, 'As in his previous hit about psychiatry,
*Blue/Orange*, Penhall shows a subtle feel for big issues in small
settings.' Indeed, the 'small' setting of the consultation room
enables Penhall's play to explode outwards; by maintaining
focus on the situation, arguments and developments in plot
and character, the 'big issues' can be tackled through dialogue,
proxemics and specific physicality rather than through shifting
space or architecture. The audience come to understand the
institutional structures which are at work in this hospital
through a detailed exploration of just three characters and
their interactions. In a 'Platform Interview' at the National
Theatre on 15 May 2007, Penhall described his approach to
his craft, saying that he is 'interested in making as many
vibrations as possible with as little as possible'. That is, he tends
to set his plays in relatively contained spaces, focusing on
character development and dialogue. Indeed, this feature of

his work is so consistent that, in her review of *Landscape with Weapon* for the *Observer*, Susannah Clapp opened by calling for a reconsideration, saying:

> Joe Penhall's plays (the most celebrated is the psychiatrically based *Blue / Orange*) are seldom exactly what they seem. Their subjects are sober, but their dialogue is buoyant with jokes. They are so full of dilemma and argument that they might be issue dramas, but their true strength is in the study of character.

## Structure

As well as having a single setting, *Blue / Orange* takes place over the course of just twenty-four hours. As mentioned earlier, Penhall had been working on the ideas for *Blue / Orange* on and off for a number of years, but the piece as it now stands was written, according to Penhall, in three weeks at the end of 1999, after he directed a rehearsed reading of the American playwright David Mamet's *Speed-the-Plow* (1988). Penhall has mentioned Mamet's work in several interviews, claiming that working on this three-act, three-character play enabled him to develop his own play's structure. William C. Boles says that Penhall 'retained two characters from his original script – Bruce, a young doctor, and Christopher, a black patient – and then crafted a new one, Robert, a senior doctor' (*The Argumentative Theatre of Joe Penhall*, p. 115).

Mamet's play is a brutal satire on Hollywood and the film industry, so at the content level, the two plays have little in common. But the play's three-act structure in which a producer, a newly promoted head of studio, and a temporary secretary engage in a battle of wills and a seemingly endless argument, over the course of a single day, is certainly echoed in *Blue / Orange*. In his review of the first production for the *Times Literary Supplement*, William McEvoy points out that, 'In the theatre, the triangulation of characters often adds up to confrontation'. He cites 'Harold Pinter's elegant geometries of emotion in *Betrayal* and *Old Times*, or Michael Frayn's in *Copenhagen*', but plenty of other examples readily suggest themselves, and it is a configuration which Penhall had used previously in *Love and Understanding*, and was to use again in *Dumb Show* and *Haunted Child*.

In a piece on Penhall's early plays, Boles cites a profile on Penhall written for the *Sunday Times* in 1998 by Simon Fanshawe, who noted that the difference between Penhall and other major young playwrights of the time had to do with Penhall's use of form and structure. As Fanshawe points out, Penhall was and remains 'a writer whose plays are unashamedly formal, even conservative in their structure, whose themes are deeply humane and who is talked about increasingly as having enough fashion-free depth to outrun the rest' (William C. Boles, 'The Rise and Fall of the Lad', p. 312). Unlike his peers – in particular, Sarah Kane, Mark Ravenhill, and Anthony Neilson – Penhall appears deliberately to reject any postmodern tropes in his use of form and style.

The structure of *Blue/Orange* is relatively straightforward, even traditional: the acts take place in real time, the piece has a linear chronology, and it is also detailed and tightly plotted. At first sight, *Blue/Orange* might seem like a wordy play: almost everything that happens takes place in, and through, dialogue. But this is not the same as saying that there is no action: its language is packed with action as the situation of the play develops. Penhall has often been called a 'dialectical' or 'argumentative' playwright, and *Blue/Orange* exemplifies this feature of his writing at its strongest. 'Dialectic' refers to a method of reasoning in which the truth is arrived at through argument and the exchange of opposing views. It is a word with a complex philosophical history, used by different thinkers in slightly different ways. Here, the most pertinent is probably Hegel's use of the term to describe a process of thought by which a thesis and antithesis (apparent contradictions) give rise to a synthesis or higher truth. In theatre, dialectic has also been used in several contexts, but in describing *Blue/Orange* in this way it is the play's use of constant and shifting argument that is highlighted. Meaning is made through the audience's understanding of the disagreement and the differing positions of the characters – principally, of course, Bruce and Robert, since Christopher, as many reviewers noted, quickly becomes a ping-pong ball for the back-and-forth of their disagreement.

This mode of playwriting might be seen to connect Penhall's work with that of an earlier generation of writers. Many of the socialist playwrights of the 1970s – including David Edgar, David Hare and Howard Brenton – used similar techniques in terms of featuring characters with very different views (often in terms of their politics) and shaping their plays using arguments between opposing positions. But Penhall's work, again, does not sit wholly comfortably here. As the play goes on, the argument between Bruce and Robert becomes increasingly muddied: rather than moving towards clarity and a fixed position or a resolution of the argument, Penhall crafts a journey towards uncertainty, complexity, and perhaps even stalemate.

*Blue / Orange*, then, commits very deliberately to a rather traditional use of structure and setting as part of its interest in the narrative and the exploration of liberalism, and as a way of effecting a shift from clear idealism to confused reality. The play crafts a set of questions and ambiguities through its dialogue and the characters' arguments, so that, although its structure is clear and straightforward, its debate is anything but simple. These questions and ambiguities stem from the uncertainties inherent in the subject matter and the characters' lack of ideological coherence about notions of moral responsibility.

## Characters and Characterisation

'I couldn't write a play about people I didn't like.'
Joe Penhall, 'Platform Interview', 7 June 2000

*Christopher*
Christopher is a twenty-four-year-old black man who has been sectioned by the police and is coming to the end of his compulsory twenty-eight days of assessment. He has been living in a small flat in west London in an area that he doesn't like, and where he feels threatened on a daily basis. We only learn a few details about his upbringing, including that he

moved around a lot as a child. His mother can't be traced, although he says that she lives in Feltham and that she came from Zaire (now part of the Congo). His father doesn't seem ever to have been around: though Christopher first claims to be the son of Ugandan dictator Idi Amin, then of legendary boxer Muhammad Ali. Although, for a while, the play holds out the possibility that the first of these claims may be true, by the close it has been revealed as an almost certain delusion. Penhall's understanding of the character that he has created is that he is, indeed, schizophrenic, and various factors (such as Christopher's delusions, and occasional references to auditory hallucinations) point towards this reading. However, it's worth recalling that in the play's initial reception there was less consensus around Christopher's diagnosis and Penhall has pointed out that, when the play is performed, it is most effective when the audience are kept unsure of Christopher's mental health for as long as possible. Christopher, like all the characters in the play, is complex – funny and belligerent; charming and threatening; brash and extremely vulnerable.

*Bruce*
Bruce is a doctor in his twenties. He is in the early years of his career, and he plans to specialise in psychiatry. He has a wife, although we learn very little about her beyond her ability to make Welsh rarebit. At the start of the play, Bruce appears well-meaning, if somewhat out of his depth. There is a tension between the rapport he seeks to build with Christopher and his rather paternalistic, occasionally patronising, behaviour towards him. There are further, more complex tensions in Penhall's portrayal of Bruce. We might see him as an idealistic young man who has faith in the health system's ability to nurture patients back to some sort of equilibrium. At the same time, his understanding that Christopher does not have a 'community' in which to be cared for suggests a more canny understanding of the system's failings, and a concern for Christopher's wellbeing. However, his outburst in Act Three – although caused by the stress of the situation – makes us ask how deep Bruce's concern really goes. In his controlling,

patronising behaviour, Bruce also echoes some of the less
popular features of the 'nanny state' which the political right
accuses the left of nurturing. His insistence that he does not
want to 'Follow the Path of Least Resistance' as instructed
(p. 25) is principled, but teeters on the edge of doggedness.
While the play is critical of the ways in which articulacy can
be misused, in Bruce we see some of the difficulties that a lack
of rhetorical flair can create. So, although he is frequently
tripped up verbally by both Robert and Christopher, Bruce
consistently demonstrates a greater understanding of the
nuances and problematics of words and their interpretation
than the others.

### Robert

Robert is a senior consultant psychiatrist. He wants to be a
professor, and is both ambitious and anxious about his career
prospects. His research into psychosis and cultural specificity
has stalled, and he therefore leaps on the chance to use
Christopher as a case study. However, when talking to him in
Act Two, he is almost incapable of focusing on what
Christopher is saying, dismissing his concerns and turning the
consultation back to himself; his judgements on Christopher's
condition therefore seem to be more flights of his imagination
than of careful clinical assessment. Like the other characters, he
is complex and sometimes paradoxical. Robert is charismatic
and occasionally charming, seeming initially to be wholly in
control of his field and its language. However, he has co-opted
the language of political correctness without really taking to
heart any of its actual meaning. While he accuses Bruce of
using racist language, it is in fact his own statements and
opinions which are more suspect. The most interesting
paradox in his characterisation lies in his seeming position as
both an establishment figure (pragmatic, following guidelines,
inflexible with the rules, authoritarian) and an anti-establishment
one (quoting Ginsberg and Laing, being whimsical and
capricious). This seeming paradox can be understood when
Robert is viewed as the incarnation of political spin: self-
serving and manipulative, he says what he needs to in order to

get his way, shifting position and argument whenever it suits the situation and with little regard for how incoherent and inconsistent this might make him appear. He appropriates the language of the counter-culture when convenient, ignoring its principles when they don't fit his own agenda.

## Staging Schizophrenia

*'One of the last great taboos'*
One of the most compelling features of Penhall's writing is that, when he is crafting characters, even the most flawed are given positions and lines that are tenable, persuasive and understandable. Thus, despite the suspicion of Robert that develops through the course of the play, his long speech about schizophrenia in which he 'joins up the dots' for Bruce remains one of its most striking moments. Robert tells Bruce that:

> Schizophrenia is the worst pariah.
> One of the last great taboos.
> People don't understand it.
> They don't want to understand it [ . . . ]
> They make *movies* about junkies and alcoholics and gangsters and men who drink too much, fall over and beat their woman until bubbles come out of her nose, but schizophrenia, my friend, is just not in the phone book.
>
> (pp. 52–3)

Bruce replies, 'Then we must change that.' As noted earlier, madness is explored in a wide range of theatre pieces and literary works. So what is Penhall's approach to staging schizophrenia, and how does it work?

Rachel Fensham's essay 'On Not Performing Madness' opens with a quotation from Yannick Ripa's *Women and Madness*, a history of French asylums and the social construction of madness in the nineteenth century, where Ripa says that:

> We should always remember that there are two ways of looking at madness: it can be observed from the outside or experienced from the inside. The difference between

experience and observation is always passed over in silence
and the hidden story of madness is never told.

Fensham (1998), p. 149

Ripa's words are a useful reminder that the observation and
representation of madness are not identical to (and may be
extremely different from) the experience of madness. In
thinking about the implications of this, it is worth contrasting
Penhall's approach to the staging and representation of mental
illness with two of the period's other significant works on
mental illness: Sarah Kane's *4.48 Psychosis* (first performed
posthumously at the Royal Court in 2000) and Anthony
Neilson's *The Wonderful World of Dissocia* (first performed at the
Tron Theatre, Glasgow, in 2004). The territory that these
three plays negotiate is somewhat different. Kane's work
explores psychosis, depression and suicide; Neilson's
protagonist Lisa has a dissociative condition; Penhall, of
course, is writing about schizophrenia. And their theatrical
strategies are also very different.

In his 'Foreword' to *The Wonderful World of Dissocia* and *Realism*
(London: Methuen Drama, 2007), Anthony Neilson says that,
'*Dissocia* was partly an attempt to theatrically represent the
internal landscape of someone who was mentally ill.' In the
first act of the play, the audience follow Lisa into 'Dissocia', a
fantastical, funny and sometimes frightening theatrical
landscape full of spectacle, imagination and increasing
outrageousness. The suggestion, as Neilson says, is that what
we experience is a representation of Lisa's 'interior'. In the
second act, there is a complete shift of style: it is the 'polar
opposite' of Act One (Neilson, p. 75). Set in Lisa's hospital
room, it is monochrome not technicolor, hyper-naturalistic not
stylised or pantomimic. Neilson's aim was to achieve a
'harmony of form and content' so that 'the entire structure of
the play was designed to force the audience into at least
analogous identification with the protagonist' (Neilson,
'Foreword').

Sarah Kane's *4.48 Psychosis* is also an attempt to match form
and content. Ariel Watson describes the play as 'a series of

meditations by an unnamed, genderless character (or possibly characters) on suicidal depression, the therapeutic relationship, psychoactive medications [ . . . ] and the moment of clarity that comes at 4.48 in the morning' (Watson, 'Cries of Fire', p. 191). The text is not allocated to speakers or characters, and is perhaps best described as fragmented and indeterminate – although its structure maps a pattern of treatment and 'care' in current psychiatric practice.

Sarah Kane and Anthony Neilson, then, are interested in the inner workings and structures of conditions and, more particularly, in finding a theatrical form that somehow fits the experience of the illness. We might say, following Ripa, that both plays attempt to explore their conditions from the inside – although we might also question how far the experience of producing or watching these pieces (which is, inevitably, an external observation) achieves this.

Joe Penhall's approach, as the discussion of the setting and structure demonstrates, is from the outside in. As Watson puts it, *Blue/Orange* is concerned – like *4.48 Psychosis* – with the failings of mental health care, but it examines 'the power structures of therapy that emerge in the act of diagnosis' (Watson, p. 189). *Blue/Orange* deals with the structures, stigma and complexity around the condition, its diagnosis and its treatment, rather than the illness itself. By focusing on the argument between Bruce and Robert, Penhall stages 'the bureaucratic doublethink of mental health care' which 'quickly emerges in *Blue/Orange* as a game of rhetorical brinkmanship that has roots in a deep anxiety about the slipperiness of language' (Watson, pp. 199–200). This is one of the reasons why so many of the play's reviewers claim not to know whether Christopher is schizophrenic or not: the play does not attempt to represent or explore his condition per se, but rather the doctors' analysis of him and his behaviour. The play is about observation and diagnosis, about language, status and power, not about the experience of living with serious mental illness. As Watson argues, Penhall's play becomes 'a potently dramatic triad of spectatorship and judgement' (p. 202) as Bruce watches Christopher, and Robert watches both Bruce and

Christopher. Further, the audience's position as observers of the whole play, attempting to follow, make sense of, and come to their own conclusions about all three characters means that *Blue/Orange* lays bare the difficulties of interpreting behaviour.

This does not mean, though, that the writer does not care about Christopher, or that he is not a well-drawn, complex character. Indeed, as my discussion of his character has indicated, he is a nuanced, often funny character, and the play works best when the audience come to understand the severity of his illness gradually, through the revelations about his delusions and hallucinations. At the same time, there are many moments where Christopher's frustration and anxiety seem reasonable, comprehensible. Early in the play, he voices the desire to escape not just from the doctors, but from the present-day urban experience:

> I'm going far away where I can get some peace and quiet, no people, no cars, pollution, planes flying overhead like fruit flies, no cities, no fucking TVs, no construction work, no roadworks, no drills, no neighbours squatting on my head, under the floor, through the walls, rowing all day and night. Nothing. No people at all, man, and nobody looking at me funny like they never seen a Brother before except on fucking *Sesame Street*! I'm going far away.        (p. 21)

While Christopher is, then, ill, he is not incomprehensible, and he is frequently, as reviewers noted, the play's most likeable and sympathetic character. Perhaps this is *Blue/Orange*'s main contribution to changing and challenging some of the stigmas around mental illness.

## Race, Prejudice and Difference

As we saw earlier, *Blue/Orange* was first performed at a time when the issue of racism was very much in the public consciousness. Much of the play's action turns on the use of the phrase 'uppity nigger' and the understanding that the charge of racism is serious and potentially career-ending, and underlying concerns about continued inequality and prejudice run through the play.

Penhall hoped that the play would be a 'deconstruction of the
relatively well-meaning but nevertheless lazy assumptions that
we make about race in this country' ('Platform Interview',
7 June 2000), and he achieves this through the play's
excavation of the language of political correctness and of
articulacy. As William C. Boles says, in order to 'ensnare' the
audience in 'the play's tangled web of racist sympathies and
outrages, Penhall relies on the white, senior doctor Robert, the
glib, enticing, funny, well-spoken character. In discussing
Robert, Penhall explained that if someone comes across as
quite smart, then their racist comments go unnoticed' (*The
Argumentative Theatre of Joe Penhall*, p. 119).

Robert has an acute – if not always accurate – awareness
that race is a sensitive subject area. He is quick to jump on
Bruce's word choices, although seemingly entirely unaware
that his own attitudes are considerably more problematic. One
of the most significant exchanges in relation to the play's
interrogation of assumptions about race occurs early on, when
the two doctors discuss cultural and ethnic specificity, and the
question of 'where [Christopher] comes from' (p. 31). Boles
sums up the implications of this section, saying that:

> Robert's inability to assign the proper ethnic identity to
> Christopher, calling him 'African', presumptively and
> ignorantly assigns his home identity to an entire continent
> rather than a nationality of origin and allows him to dismiss
> Christopher's place in a British context entirely, echoing
> the same mindset of decades of politicians who refuse to
> allow blacks the full rights of their British citizenship.
>
> (Boles, p. 131)

Although Robert professes to be concerned with the ways
in which the health system is problematically ethnocentric,
he is much less able to see the nuances or particularities of
Christopher as a specific individual. It is clear to Bruce,
however, that Christopher does not have a family – much less
a community – to go back to for support (as in *Some Voices*,
illustrating some of the difficulties inherent in the movement
for 'care in the community').

As well as echoing through Robert the mindsets of many British politicians in relation to race issues, Penhall criticises a simplistic or superficial approach to race, difference and language. In *Language, Society and Power: An Introduction*, Annabelle Mooney says that: 'what is often maligned as "political correctness" may have at its heart a concern with what we could call representational justice; at least, it seems reasonable to think that language can be used such that it doesn't discriminate or demean' (p. 42). Robert is sensitive to the words used, then, but the play suggests that, though he has understood the significance of and necessity for politically correct language, though he understands the issue of institutional racism, and though his use of words has changed, his attitudes haven't: he is still discriminatory.

In terms of the language dynamics of the play, Christopher's only real power comes from his ability to use language about race, particularly words like 'nigger' and 'Brother'. If, as we shall see, the doctors constantly use medical jargon and shorthands, talking over rather than to Christopher, his way of wresting back some control is through this language: 'A what? A what. Go on, say it. An "uppity nigga"' (p. 19). Robert's attempt to see connections between Idi Amin and Muhammad Ali is tendentiously in the service of maintaining his opinions about Christopher's health (Penhall emphasises how ridiculous this is by having Christopher chime in with 'Both Muslim Fundamentalists' [p. 101] as Robert tries to list Ali and Amin's similarities). However, it is worth considering the place of these two men in relation to Christopher's character. By claiming a familial relationship with both of them, Christopher seems to be aspiring towards some of their characteristics; as the play shows Christopher's lack of control, his desire for some sort of respect and recognition becomes increasingly understandable.

## Power, Abuse and Spin

While mental health and racism are two of *Blue/Orange*'s most obvious themes, in some ways Penhall's engagement with the ideas of power – its abuse and spin – is the play's most urgent concern. In an interview with Matt Wolf, Penhall talked about being interested in writing about 'professional people abusing their position, employing power games and semantics for reasons to do with ambition'. Talking to Klein, he said that *Blue / Orange*

> is really about status and how the medical profession is like any other. It was just saying that in this country we pay too much attention to the well-spoken, well-educated individual. [ . . . ] Every profession – the dental, the acting, the legal probably more than any other – has its cowboys and charlatans. Like Bernard Shaw's *The Doctor's Dilemma*, *Blue / Orange* is about the conspiracy of the professions against the laity, the educated establishment against those who have no status at all.                                    (p. 85)

At the start of the play, it seems that Bruce at least has Christopher's best interests and his health at heart. And it seems that the argument between Bruce and Robert is to do with pragmatism and a difference in diagnosis. However, Robert gradually reveals himself to be self-interested – as the start of Act Two aptly demonstrates. Indeed, through Robert, Penhall creates an epitome and then a searing critique of 'spin'. Invited to talk about this by Klein, Penhall replied:

> Spin is something that began in the Thatcher era and was wholeheartedly adopted by Blair. A brilliant talent for manipulating words, and making dangerous things sound innocuous. What characterised the Labour government in England prior to Blair was that they were not especially manipulative or big on advertising campaigns, twisting the truth, whereas the Conservative government were. [ . . . ] This changed in the 1990s when they decided they had better become brilliant at public relations and adept propagandists. In other words, more manipulative. At first it seemed a good thing. But subsequently it disintegrated, started to become propaganda, to become untruthful.
>                                                                          (p. 81)

While Robert's first moments on stage during the first act –
in which he ignores Christopher entirely – are telling, the
argument between Bruce and Robert sounds like a case of
naivety versus experience. But embedded in this conversation
is evidence that Robert's rhetorical strategy is simply to use
whatever argument serves his purpose best at that moment.
Thus, he first offers managerial reasons for Christopher's
discharge, then differing diagnoses, then anti-psychiatry
rhetoric. Regardless of whether discharging Christopher is the
best thing for him (the argument about the relative risks for
Christopher of release into a community that doesn't exist,
versus the risks of becoming institutionalised if he remains in
hospital, is almost irresolvable), this shifting of position is
troubling, and sets the groundwork for the later acts. He co-
opts language, ideas and arguments with no regard for their
integrity, whether they are compatible, or whether he is
contradicting himself. Indeed, between Acts One and Three,
Penhall neatly shows Robert performing a complete U-turn,
from saying 'my semantics are better than yours so I win'
(p. 28) to 'OK, all right, whatever the *fucking semantics*, it was
an unfortunate incident' (p. 100).

By the end of the play, it is unclear whether anyone has
Christopher's interests in mind, let alone at heart. Christopher,
sounding increasingly confused by the doctors as much as by
his illness, exclaims, 'I don't know what to think any more.
When I do think, it's not my thoughts, it's not my voice when
I talk. [ . . . ] I don't know who I am any more!' (p. 102). Both
doctors' responses reiterate their own positions about whether
Christopher should stay in hospital or go home, almost on top
of each other. Indeed, in the first production, the actors, who
were positioned on either side of Christopher, simply shouted
over one another, vying for Christopher's attention. Visually
and aurally, it was clear that Christopher was being fought
over, not cared for.

But if, by the end of the play, we question both doctors'
motives and principles, it is very clear that it is Robert whose
position is the more problematic and even dangerous. At the
end of the play, he says that:

You see, sick people come to me.
All creeds and colours.
They are suffering.
They go away again and they no longer suffer.
Because of me.
All because of me.
And there's nothing wrong with that.
Is there?                                           (p. 115)

There are plenty of examples of Robert's inflated sense of self
throughout the play – most obviously his exasperated statement
to Bruce that 'most young doctors' would 'lick [his] anus' for
the chance to be supervised by him, and his statement that
'I am the Authority' (p. 52) – but in these closing lines of the
play, Penhall removes any question over whether or not Robert
is credible. Even without a detailed knowledge of psychiatry, it
is clear that his statement (which, as Bruce points out, suggests
a sense of godlike omnipotence) is ridiculous. 'What I'm
writing about in this play,' Penhall said in an interview with
Brian Logan, 'is the arrogance and self-assurance of bourgeois
liberalism. I think you can take it as read that those in positions
of authority are almost invariably inadequate.' By the end of
the play, though, Robert seems to be not just inadequate but
also worryingly hubristic.

## Language

*'My semantics are better than yours'*
As noted throughout this commentary, at the heart of
Blue/Orange is a battle over words, meaning and understanding
in which language is used as a weapon, is shown to be slippery
and problematic, and in which questions are asked about
whose words are listened to.

Through all his plays, but particularly in Blue/Orange,
Penhall has shown himself to be extremely skilful at writing
dialogue. At first sight, he creates realistic dialogue patterns
using repetition, hesitation, qualification. However, his aim is
not solely – perhaps not even principally – to mimic the
patterns of everyday speech. When discussing his writing, he

has referred to his experience as a journalist of transcribing speech, and also of the influence of surrealist writers such as Beckett and Ionesco (see Aragay, p. 86). He is interested, then, in the surrealism of everyday speech, and also, as he puts it, in developing a kind of 'heightened naturalism' and 'poetic realism' (interview with Aleks Sierz, 2005).

In order to shape his three characters in *Blue/Orange*, he uses a range of linguistic registers – including medical jargon, cultural references, colloquialisms, and the language of anti-psychiatry – in order to demonstrate the ways in which power operates in institutions. The doctors frequently use the language of their profession to speak over Christopher, and it's one of the recurring features of the play that Christopher is left trying to use and gain some sort of control over his situation by repeating things that have been said to him.

When considering the place of language in *Blue/Orange*, as well as thinking about the ways in which Penhall crafts dialogue it's important to note that the play explores a set of anxieties about the ways in which language relates to reality. This is partially reflected in Penhall's use of the psychiatric profession, where diagnoses are based on observation and the interpretation of behaviour in relation to a set of diagnostic criteria. Language – and shared understandings of it – are clearly of huge significance, as when Bruce and Robert argue over whether Christopher has BPD or schizophrenia.

Although the doctors only occasionally listen to Christopher's own descriptions of his experiences, *Blue/Orange* is deeply concerned with the role of language in identifying, describing and communicating our perceptions of reality. Thus, as well as paying attention to when precisely a character is in control of the play's language and dialogue, *Blue/Orange* also asks us to think about the ways in which language is interpreted. Further, Penhall's interest in cultural specificity and the anxiety that the characters have in the play about the words that they are 'allowed' to use – 'we don't say "black" any more', says Robert; 'Yes we do', retorts Bruce (p. 50) – means that *Blue/Orange* is a particularly interesting play to consider alongside debates about both the politics and the limitations of language.

## Production History and Reception

*Blue / Orange* was, according to Joe Penhall, one of two plays that he offered to the National Theatre in the late 1990s. As he said in an interview with Jasper Rees for the *Daily Telegraph* in 2001, 'One had lots of scenes, lots of characters, lots of story, it was very big and had a bit of everything. The other had three blokes and an orange.' The first production of *Blue / Orange*, with Chiwetel Ejiofor playing Christopher, Andrew Lincoln as Bruce and Bill Nighy playing the part of Robert (which Penhall had written with the actor in mind), opened at the National's Cottesloe Theatre in April 2000, directed by Roger Michell. Nearly 90,000 tickets were sold over the course of its initial run, and it was noted as a triumph for the National, which, according to both Michael Billington in the *Guardian* and Sheridan Morley in the *Spectator*, was experiencing a relatively poor run in terms of new plays, especially when compared to the successes of venues such as the Royal Court over the same period.

In an interview with Liz Leek published in the National Theatre's education pack for *Blue / Orange*, Michell explained the inspiration for the production's set design. He said that the design team 'worked in depth on the idea of institutions. We visited a nineteenth-century lecture theatre at Guy's Hospital and were struck by the intensity of focus that was created by the "tiering" of the seats – hence our boxing ring' (p. 4). In William Dudley's design the Cottesloe space was configured so that the performance took place in the round, with the audience on steeply raked seats. A number of reviewers commented on the impression of the boxing ring and the verbal sparring match between the characters. Joan Fogel, reviewing the play for *Pendulum 2000: The Journal of the Manic Depression Fellowship* (Vol. 16, No. 2), also wondered whether the square staging area surrounded by audience members 'was an intentional symbol of trying to fit a square peg into a round hole'.

Of course, one of the main difficulties with performing in the round lies in the way that the actors and set will almost inevitably block the action for at least some of the spectators, at least for part of the time. In the case of *Blue/Orange*, though, this difficulty chimed effectively with the play's preoccupation with subjectivity, bias and interpretation. Further, as William McEvoy's review for the *Times Literary Supplement* noted, the staging became particularly effective in the third act, as when Bruce loses his temper with Christopher and 'only half the audience can see Bill Nighy eavesdropping in the consultation room doorway. Where we are affects how much we know.' McEvoy also discussed the effect of the staging in relation to the fact that the audience was, by virtue of surrounding the stage, visible to itself, so that 'in a play which questions limits of every kind, the border between who is watching and being watched, judging and being judged, also becomes permeable' (24 April 2000, p. 20). This might remind us of Ariel Watson's analysis of *Blue/Orange* and the ways in which drama about psychiatry can explore the problematics of both performing and spectating. Nicholas de Jongh's review for the *Evening Standard* suggests that 'the audience plays the role of umpire'. While picking up on the sporting language of the boxing ring, this foregrounds the way in which the back-and-forth of the argument is watched and interpreted.

William Dudley's set was extremely sparse: four identical grey chairs, a low glass table with metal legs with a glass bowl of oranges on top, and a water cooler by the set's single entrance. From a practical perspective, of course, this meant that there was little to block the audience's view. More importantly, this approach to design suggests a sensitivity towards the text and the production's understanding that this is a piece about a collision of words and personalities. Looking at the props list for this first production, the only props on stage are those which the text explicitly requires, such as the oranges, cigarettes, lighter, report and Robert's phone. The production thus maintained a focus on the performances and the arguments between the characters rather than attempting to create a fully realised hospital setting or atmosphere.

It is therefore not surprising that, along with frequent mentions of the staging, reviews of the first production tended to focus on the three performances. Many reviewers praised the skill of the actors, with Nighy garnering plaudits for his charismatic Robert. Ejiofor was awarded the Most Promising Newcomer Award for the Critics' Circle Theatre Awards 2000, and Outstanding Newcomer at the London *Evening Standard* Theatre Awards for his performance as Christopher, and was consistently picked out by reviewers for the poignancy of his performance. In the interview with Liz Leek in the National Theatre's education pack, director Michell says that they spent a lot of time working on 'making the physical characteristics of anti-psychotic drugs performable' because they 'wanted to avoid stereotypical representations of "madness" and not be reliant on slavish realism' (p. 4). Complementing Ejiofor's physicality, Nighy's performance was full of physical tics and mannerisms – from frequent glances at his watch in the first act, to chewing his cheeks when agitated, to a repeated hand movement in which he held his third and fourth fingers in his palm while gesticulating with his other two fingers and thumb.

The time intervals between the acts were signalled subtly in the design: in Act Two, the lighting was considerably dimmer, with softly focused spotlights on the two actors' chairs and the bowl of oranges, suggesting that it taks place much later, but we were reminded that it is still the same day by Christopher and Robert wearing the same costumes as in Act One (though Robert has taken off his jacket and rolled up his sleeves, looking simultaneously rather more dishevelled and relaxed). Act Three looked much like Act One, but all the characters had now changed into different clothes.

Running at two hours fifteen minutes (including one interval), Michell said that the production 'cut somewhere between twenty and thirty minutes of text during rehearsal', with Penhall's support and agreement. Although some of the more detailed lines about Robert's research – particularly the section in Act One about his PhD – were cut, the omissions were mostly line-pruning rather than excisions of any significant element. Additionally, the production especially in its first act was exceptionally pacey, with characters frequently talking over one another. The effect of this, of course, was first and foremost to make the conversation sound realistic but, at the same time when lines overlap the audience are rendered less likely to hear or register every single word. Meaning, then, comes as much from pace, intonation and how the actors use their bodies as from gleaning all the details of their speech. This effect was most famously and innovatively used in Caryl Churchill's play, *Top Girls* (1984), especially in the first act where six characters at a dinner party conduct multiple overlapping conversations; and Penhall – like many other contemporary British writers – has voiced his admiration of Churchill's writing. The variations in pace also helped the production ensure that, right from the start, the play was laced with tension.

In terms of the way that the piece was publicised and marketed, its first poster and programme cover are noteworthy. The design uses a series of pictures by Bryan Charnley called *Self Portrait*. Charnley had schizophrenia and painted this series over three months in 1991 while altering the mixture and dosage of drugs on which he depended (he also kept a diary to be read alongside these paintings). He committed suicide ten days after completing the series, having taken no medication for over a month. His paintings, now held at the Prince of Wales International Centre for SANE research in Oxford visually communicate some of the experiences of extreme mental illness while at the same time attesting to the difficulty and potential limitations of attempting to do so. In his diary entry for 23 May, alongside a self-portrait in blue which shows him with a mouth in his forehead (Charnley was increasingly suffering delusions about broadcasting), he wrote:

I really tire of having to explain my paintings. It is very much my tragedy that people cannot understand the straightforward poetic use of symbols I am employing. [ . . . ] One is very much up against the almost impossible task of describing in paint that which is essentially totally invisible. Symbols come to be employed and the appropriate one must be found, also it should have a poetic charge attached to it. Yet still people are too ignorant to see.

The programme contained a quotation from Ralph Ellison's novel *Invisible Man* (1952), an extract from Büchner's play *Woyzeck* (1837), the opening of Ginsberg's long poem *Howl* (1956), the full French text of Paul Éluard's poem 'La terre est bleue comme une orange', and a quotation from R. D. Laing about the way that 'Society values its normal man.' It also included Robert's speech about schizophrenia and statistics from a study of 450 people with mental health problems carried out in February 2000 by the National Schizophrenia Fellowship. These suggest that African-Caribbean men are up to twelve times more likely to receive a diagnosis of schizophrenia than white men, while statistics also reveal significant discrepancies in treatment (for example, that '72% of black respondents had been forcibly restrained compared with 39% of white respondents'). The survey also declares that 'the NSF does not accept that any individual ethnic group has greater inherent susceptibility to severe mental illness than any other groups'.

This contextual and educative material points to the play's status as an issue-led piece, and also explicitly highlights the production's engagement with the broader contexts and issues. However, it's worth noting that the extracts and statistics are inserted without editorial or explanatory notes; they appear alongside one another for the reader to make connections between them, and between them and the play. We might regard this either as a way of allowing the audience to come to their own conclusions and do their own thinking or, perhaps, as a way of adding more material but little more sense or argument to an already packed play.

On the whole, the production was extremely well liked by reviewers, although it is worth noting that their interpretations varied considerably (revealing as much about the reviewers, perhaps, as about Penhall's work), and some were concerned about whether the play and its production were credible or realistic. Alongside Ejiofor's awards, the play and production won two of the most significant awards in the British theatre world: the 2000 *Evening Standard* Best Play Award and the London Critics' Circle Best New Play Award. A year after its first performance, it transferred with the same cast to the

Duchess Theatre in the West End. Here the theatre space was reconfigured to enable William Dudley's set to be re-created (the Duchess has a fixed proscenium arch, whereas the Cottesloe was designed for flexible staging). By this point the production imagery had changed to a photograph of the three characters lying on the floor (all of them smoking), in a triangular head-to-toe formation, around the set's glass table with its bowl of oranges. Again, the production was well received, and *Blue/Orange* won the Laurence Olivier Award for Best New Play in 2001. In September 2001 a change of cast at the Duchess saw David Threlfall replacing Bill Nighy as Robert, Neil Stukie taking the role of Bruce, and Shaun Parkes playing Christopher.

Since then, *Blue/Orange* has been revived numerous times both nationally and internationally. In 2005 Kathy Burke directed the play at the Crucible, Sheffield, with Jimmy Akingbola as Christopher, Shaun Evans as Bruce, and Roger Lloyd Pack as Robert, in a production on a thrust stage in a design which reviewers praised for its bleak, monochrome colour scheme. This production toured to Northampton, Brighton and Cambridge. There was a production at Bolton Octagon in 2006, directed by Mark Babych, while in November 2007, Tim Luscombe's version of the play was performed at the New Victoria Theatre, Newcastle-under-Lyme; in 2008 there came a touring version by Plain Clothes Theatre Company, taken to venues around the south east of England; and in 2012 the Theatre Royal, Brighton, produced a a touring production directed by Christopher Luscombe. All too often in Britain new plays are not professionally revived so soon after their first production, and it is a considerable tribute to Penhall's work and the play's strengths that it saw so many productions all over the country in the decade following its first performance.

The first revival in London of *Blue/Orange* was at London's Arcola Theatre in October 2010. Produced by the African theatre company Tiata Fahodzi, and directed by Femi Elufowoju Jr, this version was noteworthy for several reasons. The company's main intervention into Penhall's text was a gender reversal of all the characters: Ayesha Antoine played Juliet (Christopher), Esther Hall played Emily (Bruce) and Helen Schlesinger played Hilary (Robert). The experiment was an interesting one, if only partially successful. It threw up questions about gender construction and whether Penhall's script is only, or principally, to do with masculinity. The production tended to falter in the quality and precision of the directing and acting, and (as Dominic Maxwell's review for *The Times* pointed out) Hilary/Robert seemed to be a much more awkward gender swap than the other characters, which had knock-on problems in terms of the shape and sense of all the characters' frustrations. However, the reviewers unanimously felt that, 'nothing much has dated in this depiction of an NHS bound up in doublespeak and limited resources' (Maxwell, *The Times*, 5 November 2010) and that Penhall's play felt as urgent as it had a decade earlier. The third point of particular interest here was the set design by Ultz. In the Arcola's low-ceilinged main space, the audience were seated on three sides of a walled consultation room. Windows from waist height allowed us to look into the room, emphasising the audience's position as 'voyeurs, sometimes sucked into vivid engagement yet often estranged by the prolixity of the arguments being set before us' (Henry Hitchings, *Evening Standard*, 5 November 2010).

Given that *Blue/Orange* is set explicitly in a UK context, with reference to a specific care system and situated in a precise political and artistic context, it might seem slightly surprising that it has also been performed across the world. However, aspects of the play are clearly capable of travelling – particularly, as previously discussed, in relation to the broader contexts of the use of madness as a literary trope, and, of course, in its exploration of power and politicking. In the United States, it was first presented Off Broadway by the Atlantic Theater Company in late 2002, directed by Neil Pepe. In Germany, where many contemporary British plays are performed, its first production was in Essen in 2001, directed by Jürgen Bosse.

As well as all of these stage versions of the play, *Blue/Orange* has also been adapted, by Penhall, for television. First aired on

BBC Four in 2005, the ninety-minute piece starred Shaun
Parkes as Christopher (who had played the role on stage in
2001), John Simm as Bruce, and Brian Cox as Robert. It was
directed by Howard Davies, well-known for his work in both
television and theatre, who has directed many pieces by writers
such as David Hare and Michael Frayn. In the transition to
television, a number of alterations were made, none of which
was substantial but some of which are worth noting. In
particular, all the references to Bruce's wife were cut, as were
references to the rugby match that, in the stage play, the two
doctors have attended together.

Unlike the stage version, the television production does not
remain solely in one room. The piece opens with shots of the
three characters before the play starts: Bruce on his bike,
Robert in an open-top car, and Christopher in his hospital
room, shadow-boxing in front of a picture of Muhammad Ali.
Of course, we must bear in mind here the different conventions
of theatre and television, the different possibilities of each
medium, and the rather different ways in which an audience's
attention is held – in theatre, lengthy set changes risk being
tedious, while in television a single location might quickly
become boring. In Act One, for example, the dialogue takes
place in a hospital consultation room, in an outside area (a
simple reversion of the play – rather than sending Christopher
out, the doctors leave the room), in Chris's room, in the
hospital canteen and in Robert's office. There are also several
moments where the camera cuts away from Bruce and Robert
so that we hear their conversation, but see Christopher.

In the gap between Acts Two and Three, we see Robert
typing something (which we then, of course, realise is the
report) late at night, before seeing Bruce cycling to work the
next day and being given a stack of paperwork which includes
the report. In this sequence, we also see Christopher doing a
jigsaw, and we see and then hear Muhammad Ali on the
room's television set. In some ways, then, the television version
'fixes' or clarifies a number of things which might be more
open in stage versions of the play. At the end of the piece, we
see Christopher out on the streets of London.

Another detail worth noting is the use of sound effects. As in the first stage production, the BBC Four piece tends to be realistic – but here, this is achieved through ambient noise that might be associated with hospitals (phones ringing, receptionists, and other general background business). But the piece also uses a particular underscoring music at a number of key points: for example, when Bruce first mentions BPD; during a section where the cameras focus on Christopher throwing his belongings around his room while the two doctors, elsewhere, talk about whether or not he needs a hospital bed; towards the end of Robert's lengthy speech about schizophrenia; and at several points during the consultation between Robert and Christopher. This slightly unsettling music, which intrudes noticeably and intentionally into the soundscape, tilts the production very slightly away from straightforward television realism.

Perhaps the most striking difference between the television version of the play and its first production is in its overall tone and the impression it leaves. Both the reviews and the archive footage of the stage version suggest that the humour of the play was one of its most memorable features – indeed, Penhall said that it surprised and 'amazed me to have a large audience laughing all the way through it' ('Platform Interview' with Hemming, 7 June 2000). The television production draws rather less on the play's comedy, in part due to a different cast and the rather more sinister, less mercurial quality of Brian Cox's performance as Robert, but also no doubt due to the lack of a live audience's impact on the individual spectator's experience.

Mary O'Hara, reviewing the piece for the *Guardian* on the day of its broadcast, said that:

There was always a chance that adapting *Blue/Orange* for television would miss the target. As a stage play it worked as an almost claustrophobic examination of the relationship between just three characters: two psychiatrists and one patient. But the adaptation cleverly and sensitively focuses on how disagreements between doctors over how to treat

their patient reflects on the system as a whole. [ . . . ]
Psychiatric practitioners may or may not see similarities
with their own working lives, but for the uninitiated, the
programme should provoke some serious reflection on how
mental health conditions are diagnosed and treated.

In her final paragraph she pointed to the piece's wider aims
and concerns:

For those people who are disillusioned by the approaching
general election, tonight's programme should be a shot in
the arm. Penhall's play is a timely and provocative reminder
of why policy matters, and of how politics affects the lives
of some of society's most vulnerable people.

Despite its specificities of time, place and context – or perhaps,
in part, because of them – *Blue / Orange* has, then, proved to be
one of the most performed plays of the past twenty years.
That it has done so tells us about the continued significance
of issue-led, argument-driven plays in the British theatre.
However, as O'Hara suggests, its impact lies as much in its
underlying arguments about language, power, politics and
policy as it does in its explicit points about race and mental
health.

# Further Reading

## Works by Joe Penhall

PLAYS

*Plays: One* (*Some Voices*, *Pale Horse*, *Love and Understanding*, *The Bullet*). London: Methuen Drama, 1998.
*Plays: Two* (*Blue/Orange*, *Dumb Show*, *Wild Turkey*). London: Methuen Drama, 2008.
*Landscape with Weapon*. London: Methuen Drama, 2007.
*Haunted Child*. London: Methuen Drama, 2011.
*Birthday*. London: Methuen Drama, 2012.

FILMS

*Blue/Orange*. Dir. Howard Davies. BBC Wales, 2005.
*Moses Jones*. Dir. Michael Offer. BBC, 2009.
*The Road*. Dir. John Hillcoat. Dimension Films, 2009.
*Some Voices*. Dir. Simon Dellan Jones. Dragon Pictures, 2000.
*The Long Firm*. Dir. Bille Eltringham. BBC Drama Group, 2004.
*The Undertaker*. Dir. Joe Penhall. BBC Films, 2005.

## Selected Interviews

Aragay, Mireia, Hildegard Klein, Enric Monforte and Pilar Zozoya (eds), *British Theatre of the 1990s: Interviews with Directors, Playwrights, Critics and Academics*. Basingstoke: Palgrave Macmillan, 2007. [Contains a lengthy interview with Penhall, covering a range of his plays.]
Devine, Harriet, *Looking Back: Playwrights at the Royal Court, 1956–2006*. London: Faber, 2006.
Hemming, Sarah, 'It's a Mad, Mad, Mad, Mad World'. *Independent*, 12 April 2000.
Logan, Brian, '"If You've Got a Big Mouth, the Stage is the Place to Be"'. *Guardian*, 12 April 2000.

Penhall, Joe, 'Platform' on *Blue/Orange*, chaired by Sarah
    Hemming. Cottesloe Theatre, National Theatre, London,
    7 June 2000.
————— , 'Platform' on *Landscape with Weapon*, chaired by
    Aleks Sierz. Cottesloe Theatre, National Theatre, London,
    15 May 2007.
Rees, Jasper, 'Vexed Questions of Colour'. *Daily Telegraph*,
    30 April 2001.
Sierz, Aleks, theatrevoice.com, 31 January 2005.
Wolf, Matt, 'Power Games that Scar in a Psychiatric Arena'.
    *New York Times*, 24 November 2002.

*Reviews of Penhall's plays can be found in many newspapers' online archives, or collected in* London Theatre Record.

## Secondary Sources

PENHALL AND BRITISH THEATRE

Billington, Michael, *State of the Nation: British Theatre Since
    1945*. London: Faber, 2007. [The final chapter contains a
    brief mention of *Blue/Orange*, but it positions it within the
    broader (mainstream) theatre context and some wider
    social/political context.]
Boles, William C., *The Argumentative Theatre of Joe Penhall*.
    Jefferson, NC, and London: McFarland, 2011. [The first
    monograph on Penhall's work, this contains a detailed
    chapter on *Blue/Orange*.]
————— , 'The Rise and Fall of the Lad: Joe Penhall's Early
    Plays'. In *Drama and the Postmodern: Essays Assessing the Limits
    of Metatheatre*, ed. Daniel Jernigan (Amherst, NY: Cambria
    Press, 2008), pp. 307–25.
Dromgoole, Dominic, *The Full Room: An A–Z of Contemporary
    Playwriting*. London: Methuen Drama, 2000.
Kritzer, Amelia Howe, *Political Theatre in Post-Thatcher Britain:
    New Writing: 1995–2005*. London: Palgrave, 2008. [Chapter 2
    contains a section on Penhall's work, focusing on *Some Voices*
    and *Blue/Orange*.]
Leek, Liz, *NT Education Workpack: Blue/Orange*. London: National
    Theatre, 2001.
    <www.nationaltheatre.org.uk/download.php?id=4430>

Littler, Ruth, and Emily McLaughlin, *The Royal Court Theatre Inside Out*. London: Oberon Books, 2007. [Contains a handful of references to Penhall's work, including sections on *Some Voices* and *Pale Horse*.]

Middeke, Martin, Peter Paul Schnierer and Aleks Sierz (eds), *The Methuen Drama Guide to Contemporary British Playwrights*. London: Methuen Drama, 2011. [This book contains a chapter by Margarete Rubik on Penhall's work which includes and analyses of a number of his works, including *Blue/Orange*, up to *Landscape with Weapon*. It also contains chapters on a range of other key British playwrights.]

Reinelt, Janelle, 'Selective Affinities: British Playwrights at Work'. *Modern Drama* 50.3 (Fall 2007): 305–24.

Sierz, Aleks, *In-Yer-Face Theatre: British Drama Today*. London: Faber, 2000. [Chapter 8 contains a section on Penhall which focuses on *Some Voices* and provides useful information and context for Penhall's work.]

——— , *Rewriting the Nation: British Theatre Today*. London: Methuen Drama, 2011.

Watson, Ariel, 'Cries of Fire: Psychotherapy in Contemporary British and Irish Drama'. *Modern Drama* 51:2 (Summer 2008): 188–210.

PSYCHIATRY, THE ANTI-PSYCHIATRY MOVEMENT AND THE NHS

Bell, Andy, and Peter Lindley (eds), *Beyond the Water Towers: The Unfinished Revolution in Mental Health Services 1985–2005*. London: Sainsbury Centre for Mental Health, 2005.

Burns, Tom, *Psychiatry: A Very Short Introduction*. Oxford: Oxford University Press, 2006.

Foucault, Michel, *Madness and Civilization: A History of Insanity in the Age of Reason*. London: Routledge, 2001.

Frith, Christopher, and Eve Johnstone, *Schizophrenia: A Very Short Introduction*. Oxford: Oxford University Press, 2003.

Kotowicz, Zbigniew, *R. D. Laing and the Paths of Anti-Psychiatry*. London: Routledge, 1997.

Laing, R. D. *The Divided Self*. London: Penguin, 2010.

——— , *The Politics of Experience/The Bird of Paradise*. London: Penguin, 1990.

Rivett, Geoffrey. *From Cradle to Grave: Fifty Years of the NHS.*
London: King's Fund Publishing, 1998.

Saks, Elyn R., *The Center Cannot Hold: A Memoir of My
Schizophrenia.* London: Virago, 2007.

Snyder, Kurt, with Racquel E. Gur and Linda Wasmer
Andrews, *Me, Myself and Them: A Firsthand Account of One
Young Person's Experience with Schizophrenia.* Oxford: Oxford
University Press, 2007.

Timmins, Nicholas, *The Five Giants: A Biography of the Welfare
State.* Revised edn, London: HarperCollins, 2001.

———, *A History of the NHS.* London: Department of
Health, 1996.

LANGUAGE AND POWER

Mooney, Annabelle, *et al.*, *Language, Society and Power: An
Introduction.* 3rd edn, Abingdon: Routledge, 2011.

Simpson, Paul, and Andrea Mayr, *Language and Power: A Resource
Book for Students.* Abingdon: Routledge, 2010.

THEATRE, MADNESS AND MENTAL HEALTH

Feder, Lillian, *Madness in Literature.* Princeton, NJ: Princeton
University Press, 1980.

Fensham, Rachel, 'On Not Performing Madness', *Theatre Topics*
8.2 (1998): 149.

Fleming, Michael, and Roger Manvell, *Images of Madness: The
Portrayal of Insanity in the Feature Film.* London and Toronto:
Associated University Press, 1985.

Kaplan, Ellen W., and Sarah J. Rudolph (eds), *Images of Mental
Illness Through Text and Performance.* Studies in Theatre Arts,
vol. 33. Lewiston: Edwin Mellen Press, 2005.

CONTEMPORARY BRITISH POLITICS: THATCHER AND BLAIR

Evans, Eric J., *Thatcher and Thatcherism.* London: Routledge,
1997.

Gould, Philip, *The Unfinished Revolution: How New Labour
Changed British Politics Forever.* London: Abacus, 2011.

Hall, Stuart, and Martin Jacques (eds), *The Politics of Thatcherism.*
London: Lawrence and Wishart, 1983.

Kavanagh, Dennis, *Thatcherism and British Politics: The End of Consensus?* 2nd edn, Oxford: Oxford University Press, 1990.

Rawnsley, Andrew, *Servants of the People: The Inside Story of New Labour.* London: Penguin, 2001.

Riddell, Peter, *The Thatcher Era and Its Legacy.* 2nd edn, Oxford: Blackwell, 1991.

Seldon, Anthony (ed.), *Blair's Britain, 1997–2007.* Cambridge: Cambridge University Press, 2009. [See in particular Nick Bosanquet's chapter, 'The Health and Welfare Legacy', pp. 385–407.]

Seldon, Anthony, and Daniel Collings, *Britain Under Thatcher*, Harlow: Pearson Educational, 2000.

## Useful Websites

www.blackmentalhealth.org.uk/ [This website contains a range of information, statistics and news stories about mental health, aiming to address and reduce the stigma of mental illness, and in particular to reduce the inequalities in treatment and care of African-Caribbean mental health service users.]

www.inyerface-theatre.com/ [A useful resource on British theatre of the 1990s and 2000s.]

www.mentalhealth.org.uk/

www.mind.org.uk/ [Mind is one of the UK's largest mental health charities and their website is extremely informative.]

www.theatrevoice.com [There are several recorded interviews with Penhall in the archive.]

# Blue/Orange

*For my Dad,*
*the late, great Brian Penhall (1933–1998)*

*Blue/Orange* was first performed in the Cottesloe auditorium of the National Theatre, London, on 7 April 2000. The cast was as follows:

**Christopher**        Chiwetel Ejiofor
**Bruce**              Andrew Lincoln
**Robert**             Bill Nighy

*Directed by* Roger Michell
*Designed by* William Dudley

Michael Codron and Lee Dean transferred the National Theatre production to the Duchess Theatre on 30 April 2001.

**Characters**

**Christopher**
**Bruce**
**Robert**


*Setting*

The action takes place over twenty-four hours in a modern NHS psychiatric hospital in London.

# Act One

*A consultation room. A transparent water cooler. A round table with a large glass bowl containing three oranges.*

**Bruce** *and* **Christopher** *stand facing each other.*

**Christopher**   Mister Bruce –

**Bruce**   Christopher –

**Christopher**   Mister Bruce –

**Bruce**   How are you doing?

**Christopher**   Brucey Brucey Brucey. How you doing?

**Bruce**   A pleasure as always.

**Christopher**   A pleasure. Yeah, a pleasure. The pleasure's all mine, man.

**Bruce**   Take a seat.

**Christopher**   The pleasure today is mine. D'you know what I mean?

**Bruce**   Plant your arse.

**Christopher**   It's mine! It's my day. Innit. My big day. What can I say . . . ?

**Bruce**   Yes, well, yes – sit down now.

**Christopher**   Gimme some skin.

**Bruce**   Why not.

**Bruce** *shakes* **Christopher***'s hand.* **Christopher** *makes it an elaborate one. They punch fists.*

**Christopher**   I'm a free man. D'you know what I mean?

**Bruce**   Well . . . aha ha . . . OK.

**Christopher**   I'm a happy man. Bursting with joy.

**Bruce**   Chris?

**Christopher**    Oh – hey – oh . . . OK. I'll be good. You're right. I should sit.

**Christopher** *sits with exaggerated calm.*

**Bruce**    Relax.

**Christopher**    I should relax and calm myself.

**Bruce**    Take a few breaths. Would you like some water?

**Christopher** (*fidgeting*)    Uh?

**Bruce**    Would you like a cup of water?

**Christopher**    Coke.

**Bruce**    No, you can't have –

**Christopher**    Ice-cold Coke. The Real Thing.

**Bruce**    No, you know you can't have Coke –

**Christopher**    Yeah I can because –

**Bruce**    What did I tell you about Coke?

**Christopher**    I'm going home tomorrow.

**Bruce**    What's wrong with drinking Coke?

**Christopher**    But I'm going home.

**Bruce**    Chris? Come on you know this, it's important. What's wrong with Coke?

*Pause.*

**Christopher**    It rots your teeth.

**Bruce**    No – well, yes – and . . . ? What else does it do to you?

**Christopher**    Makes my head explode.

**Bruce**    Well – no – no – what does it do to you really?

**Christopher**    Makes my head explode – oh man – I know – I get you.

**Bruce**    It's not good for you, is it?

**Christopher**    No. It's bad.

**Bruce**    What's the first thing we learnt when you came in here?

**Christopher**    No coffee no Coke.

**Bruce**    No coffee no Coke, that's right. Doesn't do us any good at all.

**Christopher**    Mm.

**Bruce**    Gets us overexcited.

**Christopher**    Yeah yeah yeah yeah, makes me jumpy.

**Bruce**    That's right so – what shall we have instead?

**Christopher**    I dunno.

**Bruce**    What would you like?

**Christopher**    What I'd really like is a Snakebite. D'you know what I mean?

**Bruce**    A Snakebite. Right, well –

**Christopher**    Cider and Red Stripe or, you know, or a rum and black or or or . . .

**Bruce**    Chris, Christopher . . . what's the rule on alcohol now?

**Christopher**    But –

**Bruce**    What's the rule on alcohol in here?

**Christopher**    Alcohol.

*Pause.*

Oh yeah. Alcohol. Heh heh. D'you know what I mean?

**Bruce**    What does alcohol do?

**Christopher**    It makes your blood thin.

**Bruce**   No . . . well, possibly, but –

**Christopher**   Makes you see things.

**Bruce**   Well . . . yes, but –

**Christopher**   See into the future maybe.

**Bruce**   Well . . . s . . . sometimes maybe but what does it mostly do?

**Christopher**   It fucks you up.

**Bruce**   It fucks you up. Precisely. How about a glass of water. Eh? Some nice cool water? From the, from the thing?

**Christopher**   Water from the thing. That's cool.

**Bruce**   Nice cool water, yes. Let me – just hold on . . .

**Bruce** *gets up and* **Christopher** *suddenly gets up too.*

**Bruce**   No no – you're all right, I'm just –

**Christopher**   No, you're all right –

**Bruce** (*sitting*)   Help yourself –

**Christopher** (*sitting*)   No no, I'll –

**Bruce**   I'll – look – this is silly.

**Bruce** *gestures.*

**Christopher**   Are you sure?

**Bruce**   Be my guest.

**Christopher** *gets up and goes to the water cooler, takes two cups, pours.*

**Bruce**   Sorted.

**Christopher** (*drinking shakily*)   Sorted for Es and whiz.

**Bruce**   . . . Indeed.

**Christopher**   Sorted, innit. Sorted for Es and whiz.

**Bruce**   Absolutely.

**Christopher** (*sitting*)   D'you know what I mean? Heh heh. You must know what I mean? Eh? Eh? *Doctor.*

*He puts a cup of water in front of* **Bruce** *and sips his own.*

**Christopher**   D'you know what I mean?

**Bruce**   Huh. Of course . . .

**Christopher**   D'you know what I mean?

**Bruce**   Well . . .

*Pause.*

No. I don't.

**Christopher**   Yeah you do.

**Bruce** *sips his water.*

**Christopher**   Where's the *drugs*, man?

**Bruce**   . . . Oh the *drugs*. Of course . . .

**Christopher**   It's all that, innit. 'Where's the drugs, man? Oh man, these patients giving me massive big headache, man, massive big headache, what have I got in my doctor's bag, gimme some smack, where's some smack? Where's the Tamazie Party? This bad nigga patient I got. This *bad nigga dude* I know. My God! I Can't Take The Pressure!' Innit? Innit. Go home to the old lady – 'Aw I can't take the pressure. Oh no. I can't calm down. Oh no – yes – no – I can't shag until you gimme the smack, darling!' D'you know what I mean? Ha ha ha ha ha. Oh no. Ha ha. It's all that. You with me?

*Pause.*

**Bruce**   Well . . .

**Christopher**   Yeah yeah . . . go on! Typical white doctor. This is how *white* doctors speak: 'Drugs? What drugs? No drugs for *you*, nigga. Cos you'll only enjoy them! These are *my* drugs . . .'

**Bruce**   It's not quite like that.

**Christopher**   Deny. It's all you doctors do! Deny, man.

**Bruce**   Well, I don't think so really . . .

**Christopher** (*sipping water shakily*)   Bullshit. Bullshit. Why else would you do it? Why else are you here?

**Bruce**   Well, Christopher, why do you think you're here?

**Christopher**   Eh?

**Bruce**   Why are you here? Why do you think you're here?

**Christopher**   Why am I here?

**Bruce**   Yes.

*Pause.*

**Christopher**   I dunno.

**Bruce**   And you've been here a while now.

**Christopher**   Yeah – yes I have . . . that's true.

**Bruce**   Why do you think that is? If you'd just wanted drugs you wouldn't really be here, would you? You'd be out there. Scoring off somebody and . . . going home. Wouldn't you?

*Pause.*

I know I would! Eh? Ha ha. Have a smoke. Watch the football.

*Pause.*

N'ha ha.

*Pause.*

No. Obviously. I'm not a drug user – OK? You know. But joking aside – it doesn't make sense that anybody would be in here for drugs as opposed to say, you know, out there *enjoying*, enjoying their drugs. Having some fun. D'you see what I mean?

*Pause.*

I mean, they are supposed to be recreational.

*Pause.*

So my point is – and this is one of the things I want to talk to you about today – you're here to get better, aren't you? Because you've been very poorly. Haven't you?

*Long pause.*

**Christopher**    I dunno.

**Bruce**    Ah.

**Christopher**    What's up? I'm going home. You should be happy.

**Bruce**    Well, I'm not as happy as you.

**Christopher**    I been saying all along, there's nothing wrong with me and now you agree with me and, I just, I just, I just . . . I'm going home.

*Pause.*

I don't know why I'm here.

*Pause.*

It's mad, innit. It's bonkers. Mad shit. First thing I said when I arrived. When I first come in here. I had a look, I saw all the all the, you know, the others, the other geezers and I thought . . . Fuck This. My God! These people are insane! Ha ha ha ha ha . . . Get Me Outta Here –

**Bruce**    Ha ha yes –

**Christopher**    It's a *nut*house, man.

**Bruce**    I grant you – indeed – there are a fair proportion –

**Christopher**    A *fair proportion*? You're kidding me.

**Bruce**    Of quite, quite –

**Christopher**    They are NUTS!

**Bruce**    . . . crazy people here . . . yes –

**Christopher**    Crazies, man! Radio Rental.

**Bruce**    People with – well – we don't actually use the term 'crazy' . . .

**Christopher**    You just said it.

**Bruce**    I know I just said it but – I shouldn't have – I was – humouring – I was, you know – it's a no-no.

**Christopher**    But you just said it.

**Bruce**    I know, but – you see my point?

**Christopher**    You said it first.

**Bruce**    OK, look . . . there are things we . . . there are terms we use which people used to use all the time, terms which used to be inoffensive but things are a bit different now. Certain words.

**Christopher**    Certain words, what words?

**Bruce**    Just . . . terms which aren't even that offensive but –

**Christopher**    Same as I say, what's offensive about it?

**Bruce**    Well –

**Christopher**    It's true!

**Bruce**    It's not true . . . it's – OK – it's not even that – it's just inaccurate. Some terms are just inaccurate. 'Crazy' is one of them. It's just . . . unhelpful. Woolly.

**Christopher**    'Woolly'. Oh. OK. I'm sorry.

**Bruce**    For example, people used to say 'schizophrenic' all the time. 'Such-and-such is schizophrenic.' Because it's two things at once. OK. Used to denote a divided agenda, a dual identity, the analogy of a split personality. Except we know now that schizophrenia doesn't mean that at all. Split personality? Meaningless. OK? So it's an unhelpful term. It's inaccurate. What we call a 'misnomer'. And this is a sensitive subject. We must think carefully, be *specific*. Because it's too . . . you know . . . it's too serious.

*Pause.*

You were diagnosed with 'Borderline Personality Disorder'. What does that mean?

*Pause.*

Borderline personality disorder. OK? Key word – *borderline*. Because, clinically speaking, you're on the *border* between neurotic and psychotic.

**Christopher**    Just . . . on the border.

**Bruce**    Yes. And that's a very useful term, isn't it? Because if people get the word wrong – if people just get the meaning of the word wrong, how can they get the person right? How can there be any . . . any awareness? People don't know anything about it. They have stupid ideas. You lose out. So we try to 'demystify'. We try to explain.

*Pause.*

Which is what I wanted to talk to you about today. Your diagnosis. This term, this label, and what it means, because the thing is, I'm beginning to think, now . . . it's . . . well, it's a little inaccurate –

**Christopher**    YOU'VE MADE YOUR POINT I SAID I'M SORRY WHAT DO YOU WANT – BLOOD?

**Bruce**    But I'm just saying . . . in the light of recent developments –

**Christopher**    Developments? What developments. What you on about, man?

**Robert**, *carrying a cup of coffee also in a plastic cup, appears at the door and just stands there waiting.*

**Robert**    You wanted to see me.

**Bruce**    Doctor Smith. Yes, come in. Hi.

**Robert**    How's tricks?

**Bruce**    I'm fine. How are you?

**Robert**    I don't believe I've thanked you for that stupendous spread.

**Bruce**    Sorry?

**Robert**    That sumptuous meal on Saturday. After the rugby. The food.

**Bruce**    Oh. Thanks.

**Robert**    Hang on to that woman, Bruce.

**Bruce**    Sure.

**Robert**    You'll live to a hundred and three.

**Bruce**    The thing is –

**Robert**    The only woman I know with the audacity to pull off a fondue. I thought, 'Any minute now she'll be climbing into her caftan.'

**Bruce**    It was Welsh rarebit.

**Robert**    Welsh rarebit? The very thing.

**Bruce**    I know it's not what you're used to –

**Robert**    On the contrary. It was just the ticket. Miserable and wet. Vanquished by the Frog and foot-sore.

**Bruce**    Well, it soaked up the booze.

**Robert**    I couldn't believe that score. Not from the Frogs. Still, at least it wasn't Australia –

**Bruce**    Doctor Smith –

**Robert**    Or New Zealand or any of the other hairy colonial outposts.

**Bruce**    Doctor –

**Robert**    Welsh rarebit, eh? Took me back to my student days. Tie that woman to the nearest bed and inseminate her at once.

**Bruce**    Doctor –

**Robert**    *Breed*. Lots of little Bruces. Have you thought any more about that loft conversion? All the rage when I was a student. Quite the thing for somebody in your circumstances.

**Robert** *winks at* **Christopher** *conspiratorially and* **Christopher** *just stares back blankly.*

**Bruce**    Doc –

**Robert**    That'll set you back a few quid. Still, when you become a consultant . . .

**Bruce**    D –

**Robert**    That's where the big bucks are.

**Bruce**    The thing is –

**Robert** (*to* **Christopher**)    Hello.

**Bruce**    You remember Christopher? Chris, do you remember Doctor Smith? Senior Consultant.

**Christopher**    Warning warning warning! Alien life form approaching, Will Robinson.

**Robert**    Mm, ha ha ha –

**Bruce**    Mm, yes –

**Robert**    Very witty –

**Bruce**    OK . . . look –

**Christopher**    Warning warning warning . . . d'you know what I mean?

**Bruce**    Let's not get too distracted.

**Robert**    I'm distracting you of course.

**Bruce**    No no, you –

**Robert**   I –

**Bruce**   I want you to –

**Robert**   Well, of course, you asked me to –

**Christopher**   D'you know what I mean?

**Bruce**   I've asked Doctor Smith to sit in today.

**Robert**   Yes that's right. Just got myself a nice cup of coffee and I'll just lurk in the corner . . .

**Christopher** (*simultaneously with 'corner'*)   Coffee . . . !

**Robert**   You won't know I'm here.

**Christopher**   He's got coffee.

**Bruce**   There's plenty of water in the –

**Christopher**   Oh wow!

**Bruce**   That's not for you.

**Christopher** (*reaching over and gesturing for coffee*)   Oh come on, man. Coffee!

**Bruce**   Chris . . . Chris . . . (*To* **Robert**.) Excuse me.

**Christopher**   I want a cup of coffee.

**Bruce**   Christopher, hey listen, that's not yours.

**Christopher**   I'll split it with you.

**Bruce**   Is that yours or isn't it?

**Christopher**   Come on, man.

**Bruce**   Chris . . . Chris, come on! What's the rule on coffee?

**Christopher** *sits and kisses his teeth.*

**Bruce**   No Coke no coffee. I'm sorry. You know why.

**Christopher**   Why?

**Bruce**   You know why.

**Christopher**    Yeah, but I get out tomorrow. I'm getting out.

**Robert**    I think your man has a point.

**Bruce** *looks at* **Robert**.

**Robert** *takes out a packet of cigarettes and lights one.*

**Robert**    Sorry. I'm distracting you.

**Robert** *gets up to leave but* **Bruce** *gestures for him to sit.*

**Bruce**    Please, you aren't. Really.

**Christopher**    You got cigarettes! Gimme a cigarette, Doc, just one, I'm gagging for a puff, d'you know what I mean?

**Bruce** *nods.*

**Robert** *sits again and offers the pack to* **Christopher** *who takes a cigarette, then another, then another two, putting one behind his ear, two in his top pocket and one in his mouth.*

**Robert** *lights the cigarette for him and* **Christopher** *exhales a plume of smoke.*

**Robert**    Better?

**Christopher**    It's my nerves. I'm getting out tomorrow. You can't tell me what to do when I get out – when I'm out there – which is in (*checks his watch*) exactly twenty-four hours. I'm not under your . . . it's none of your business then, man. I'm twenty-four hours away from freedom. Out of this hole. D'you know what I mean?

*Pause.*

Forty-eight hours tops.

**Robert**    Give him some coffee, he's going home. I haven't touched mine.

**Robert** *offers the coffee,* **Christopher** *reaches for it but* **Bruce** *is there first and takes the cup, drains it in one and throws it expertly into a waste-paper bin in the corner.*

**Christopher**   Hey, man –

**Bruce**   Coffee's got caffeine in it.

**Robert**   Or a nice cup of tea?

**Bruce**   So has tea. The water's over there.

**Christopher**   What did you do that for?

**Robert**   If this isn't a good time . . . ?

**Bruce**   No, it's perfect timing. I wanted you to see this.

**Robert**   See what?

**Christopher**   I'm already *packed*.

**Bruce**   You're packed?

**Robert**   I'll just –

**Christopher**   Yeah, man. What, you think I'm not in a hurry? (*To* **Robert**.) I could use a coffee to give me a bump. Just to get me on my way, d'you know what I mean?

**Bruce**   Who said you could pack?

**Robert** (*half standing, hovering*)   Look, I can just –

**Christopher**   No one, man, I just did it. I just (no, you stay there), I put my pyjamas in a bag and my toothbrush in on top. (Don't move.) Took a whole five minutes. Shoot me. What, you think I 'pinched the towels' and some stationery?

**Bruce**   The thing is . . .

**Christopher**   Cos I'm I'm I'm . . . I'm what?

**Robert**   I can come back –

**Christopher**   Because I'm . . . ? (No you're all right.) Cos I'm . . . ?

**Bruce**   No –

**Christopher**   I'm –

**Bruce**   No –

**Christopher**    No what? You don't even know what I was gonna say. What was I gonna say?

**Robert**    Or I can stay?

**Bruce**    No, no I wasn't –

**Christopher**    Because I'm a Brother?

*Pause.*

**Bruce** (*to* **Robert**)    Paranoia. Nihilism. Persecution. Delusion –

**Christopher**    Cos I'm an 'uppity nigga'.

**Bruce**    No. You always say that and I always tell you the same thing. No.

**Robert**    I'll come back, shall I?

**Bruce**    Doctor Smith –

**Christopher**    WOULD YOU JUST MAKE UP YOUR MIND BEFORE I GO STARK STARING BANANAS? Bouncing about like Zebedee.

**Bruce**    Christopher –

**Christopher**    Don't Christopher me, man . . . (One sip of coffee he thinks he's Batman.)

**Bruce**    You know that's not the way you talk to the consultants.

**Christopher**    He's giving me the fear.

**Bruce**    Calm down. Now you are acting like a –

**Christopher**    A what? A what. Go on, say it. An 'uppity nigga'.

**Christopher** *kisses his teeth and starts eyeballing* **Robert**.

**Bruce**    Well . . . OK, yes, frankly you are and that's not what we do, is it? Eh? And when you get out of here, if you start staring at people like that, what are they going to think?

**Christopher**   What?

**Bruce**   What are people going to think? When you get out? When you're ready . . . ?

**Christopher**   I don't fucking know.

**Bruce**   Well, what do you think they're gonna think?

**Christopher**   I don't know.

**Bruce**   They'll think you're a, a, an 'uppity nigga', that's what they'll think. Kissing your teeth. It's not you. It's silly. It's crazy. You're not a, a, a, some type of '*Yardie*' –

**Christopher**   Now you're telling me who I am?

**Bruce**   No, I'm –

**Christopher**   You're telling me who I am?

**Bruce**   I'm telling you . . . to be You.

**Christopher**   That's rum, that is. That's rich. Now I've got an identity crisis. You're a cheeky fucking monkey, you are, aren't you?

*Pause.*

**Robert**   Mm. 'Uppity' isn't strictly speaking a term we –

**Bruce** (*to* **Robert**)   Learned Unresponsiveness? Disorganised Behaviour? Decline in Social Skills? Do you get me?

**Robert**   So?

**Bruce**   Eh?

**Robert**   Look around you. *Who isn't* unresponsive, and disorganised with declining social skills? Eh? Heh heh. It's *normal.*

*Pause.*

Uh-huh huh huh.

**Bruce**   Could we have a quiet word?

**Christopher** *stands abruptly and slams his fist on the desk.*

**Christopher**    Hey! You! I'm talking to you. When I get out of this place, people won't think *anything* because I'll be gone, boy. I'm going far away where I can get some peace and quiet, no people, no cars, pollution, planes flying overhead like fruit flies, no cities, no fucking TVs, no construction work, no roadworks, no drills, no neighbours squatting on my head, under the floor, through the walls, rowing all day and night. Nothing. No people at all, man, and nobody looking at me funny like they never seen a Brother before except on fucking *Sesame Street*! I'm going far away. (What's he looking at?) Look at you – nervous as a tomcat with big balls.
D'you think I'm gonna eat you?
I might do just to see the look on your face.

**Bruce**    Nobody's looking at you funny, Chris.

**Christopher**    He is.

**Robert**    Well, are you surprised?

**Christopher**    What?

**Robert**    Are you surprised? Look at yourself. Now just . . . sit down and . . . relax, would you? Of course people stare at you when you act like this. You know that, you know what it's like.

**Christopher** *looks from one to another, kisses his teeth.*

*Pause.*

**Bruce** (*to* **Robert**)    Overburdened Nervous System. Can't look me in the eye. Thinks we're staring at him.

**Robert**    We are.

*Pause.*

**Christopher**    I'm gone, oh yes. Believe. A place with a desert. And beaches. Palm trees. Somewhere hot. D'you know what I mean?

**Bruce**   Chris . . . ? Would you mind waiting in the other room for two minutes?

**Christopher**   What did I say?

**Bruce**   Nothing at all, we just need to –

**Robert**   Consult.

**Bruce**   That's right.

**Robert**   That's why the badge says 'Consultant'. (I'm not wearing it.)

**Bruce**   Please. I'd really appreciate it. Just go through that door.

**Christopher** (*sighs*)   OK. But I hope you know what you're doing, yeah?

**Bruce**   How do you mean?

**Christopher**   I hope you're not gonna let him talk you into anything.

**Robert**   Good God no. No no no no no.

**Christopher**   Hope you're not gonna go changing your mind on me. Cos my twenty-eight . . .

**Bruce**   Chris –

**Christopher**   My twenty-eight days –

**Bruce**   I know –

**Christopher**   My twenty-eight days is up. It's up, man. You've had your fun. I'm gone. Believe.

**Bruce**   Uh-huh, OK . . . thank you.

**Christopher** *stands, lingers, stares at them both, then goes through a door.*

*Silence.*

**Bruce**   Do you think he knows?

**Robert**    What's there to know? He's a Section 2. His twenty-eight days are up. He's responded to treatment and now he's going home.

*Pause.*

Am I right?

**Bruce**    But –

**Robert**    But what?

**Bruce**    Well . . . I mean, you know what I'm going to ask you, don't you?

*Pause.*

**Robert**    What?

**Bruce**    I want a Section 3.

**Robert**    Take a deep breath, and forget you even thought of it.

**Bruce**    But –

**Robert**    Let him out. You're doing the right thing.

**Bruce**    But I'm not.

**Robert**    Yes, this is right. You are doing what is fair and right and *just* and textbook medically beneficial.

*Pause.*

And apart from anything else we don't have the beds.

**Bruce**    I'm really quite concerned –

**Robert**    Those beds are Prioritised for Emergency Admissions and Level Ones. Otherwise we'll wind up with a hospital full of long-term chronic mental patients hurtling about on *trolleys* – it'll be like the *Wacky Races*.

**Bruce**    Look –

**Robert**    There'd be scandal. They'd have my arse out of here faster than his and you'd be next. That's right. I'll never

make Professor. You'll never make your Specialist Registrar
Training. And how long did you study for that? Six years?
What were we saying on Saturday?

**Bruce**   When?

**Robert**   After the rugby. What did we talk about?

**Bruce**   I dunno, what?

**Robert**   Well, your Specialist Registrar Training. And I
said, for the coming year I am prepared to supervise you, I'll
be your 'Mentor', I'll teach you 'all I know' . . . but you have
to play the game.

**Bruce**   'Play the game'?

**Robert**   That's right. I'll push your barrow. I'll feed the
scrum but you're going to have to kick the ball into touch
once in a while.

**Bruce**   But –

**Robert**   Take my advice, if you keep your nose clean and
you enjoy psychiatry you'll almost certainly become a
consultant. Nevertheless, you don't want to be a consultant
for ever. Sooner or later you'll want to become a Senior. You
too may one day seek a professorship.

**Bruce**   If I . . . ?

**Robert**   But you can't afford to be indecisive about this.

**Bruce**   But I *am* indecisive.

**Robert**   You can't afford not to follow my advice is what I
mean.

**Bruce**   Oh, that kind of indecisive.

**Robert**   They'll close the hospital down and build another
Millennium Dome.

**Bruce**   Nobody's going to close the hospital because of one
Section 3. Are they? D'you think . . . ?

**Robert**   Yes. Perhaps.

**Bruce**   Really?

**Robert**   Yes. Perhaps.

*Pause.*

Follow the Path of Least Resistance.

**Bruce**   But . . . I can't justify throwing him out on the basis of beds.

**Robert**   You're not 'throwing him out' . . . you're doing what we are here to do. What *they* are here for us to do – and what everybody *expects* us to do.

*Pause.*

Eh? You are giving this man his *freedom*.
You are releasing this man into the bosom of the community.
You are giving him back his life.
He's going back to his people.

**Bruce**   His 'people'? He doesn't have any *people*. He doesn't have a life.

**Robert**   That's a matter of conjecture.

**Bruce**   It's true. He's on the White City Estate. It's a predominantly Jamaican community, he didn't grow up there, he doesn't know anybody and he hates it.

**Robert**   Where did he grow up?

**Bruce**   All over the place. Peripatetic childhood.

**Robert**   What about family? He must have a mother.

**Bruce**   He doesn't seem to be in contact with her any more.

**Robert**   Are you proposing to section this man again on the basis that he – what – he's lonely?

**Bruce**   It'll do his head in.

**Robert**   It'll do his head in if you section him again.

**Bruce**    He isn't ready to go. You heard him. He's unstable.

**Robert**    Borderline personality disorder. On the border of neurotic and psychotic.

**Bruce**    He was highly animated, shouting, staring.

**Robert**    You'd shout and stare if you were on the border of neurotic and psychotic.

**Bruce**    The loosening of associations? The paranoia?

**Robert**    And you can add, reckless, impulsive, prone to extreme behaviour, problems handling personal life, handling money, maintaining a home, family, sex, relationships, alcohol, a fundamental inability to handle practically everything that makes us human – and hey, Some People Are Just *Like* That. Borderline. On the border. Occasionally visits but doesn't live there. See, technically he's not *that* mentally ill. We can't keep him here. It's Ugly but it's Right.

*Pause.*

Shoot me, those are the rules.

**Bruce**    'Shoot me'? 'Some people are just like that. Shoot me'? Are you joking?

**Robert**    Deadly serious. It's what makes it so hard for us. And one day, when you're a consultant like me, and you will be, if you don't fuck this up, when every young clinician is saying exactly the same thing as you, you'll tell them what I'm telling you now. Some People Are Just Like That. Get over it. We hold their hands for twenty-eight days, wait until things have calmed down, the mess has been mopped up and off they trot, back to whatever hell they've just blown in from, usually a little bit happier and maybe even a little bit wiser until the next time.

*Pause.*

**Bruce**    Christopher is a schizophrenic.

*Pause.*

Did you hear me?

**Robert**   No, he's BPD.

**Bruce**   If you Section 3 him I can keep him here until he's properly diagnosed.

**Robert**   No. Absolutely not.

**Bruce**   He's a Type I Schizophrenic with Positive Symptoms including Paranoid Tendencies. Probably Thought Disorder as well.

**Robert**   Not Paranoid Schizophrenia?

**Bruce**   Close but I'd be loath to go that far at this –

**Robert**   It's another month before we can diagnose Schizophrenia – Paranoid or Disorganised.

**Bruce**   So resection him.

**Robert**   Is he delusional?

**Bruce**   Sometimes.

**Robert**   Since when?

**Bruce**   Since he presented.

**Robert**   How delusional?

**Bruce**   Give me time and I'll show you.

**Robert**   You haven't got time. He's been here a month. He's been steadily improving – it's therefore a brief Psychotic Episode associated with BPD. Nothing more insidious.

**Bruce**   He's paranoid. You heard him.

**Robert**   How does BPD with Paranoia sound? Stick to the ICD 10 Classification.

**Bruce**   You love the ICD 10, don't you? All the different euphemisms for 'he's nuts' without actually having to admit he's nuts. It's like your Linus blanket.

**Robert**   OK. BPD and A Bit Nuts.

**Bruce**    No. Doctor. Please.

**Robert**    'Eccentric'.

**Bruce**    Look –

**Robert**    Was he squiffy?

**Bruce**    . . . 'Squiffy'?

**Robert**    'Squiffy'. Intoxicated. When he was sectioned.

**Bruce**    . . . Yes . . . I think . . .

**Robert**    BPD with Alcoholism. It's a movable feast.

**Bruce**    What? No it's not!

**Robert**    It's a matter of 'opinion'. And I'd be loath to resection the boy on the basis of a difference of opinion. It's semantics. And right now, Doctor, my semantics are better than yours so I win.

**Bruce**    I can't live with that diagnosis.

**Robert**    *You* don't have to.

**Bruce**    I can't live with the *prognosis*.

**Robert**    Well, you can't make a new diagnosis safely for at least another month.

**Bruce**    And I can't keep him another month unless I make a new diagnosis!

*Pause.*

**Robert**    But what's he done?

**Bruce**    He hasn't done anything yet.

**Robert**    Has he tried to harm himself?

**Bruce**    No.

**Robert**    Has he tried to harm anybody else?

**Bruce**    Of course not.

**Robert**    Well, you can't section him again until he does something. Is he a danger to himself or to the public is what I'm getting at.

**Bruce**    You want to wait until he becomes dangerous?

**Robert**    We have to be sure.

**Bruce**    But we can't be sure until it's too late.

**Robert**    And we can't do anything until he does something. It's a conundrum, I know.

**Bruce**    A 'conundrum'?

**Robert**    What's the risk factor? Come on. Write it down. Pretend you're running a business.

**Bruce**    'Pretend I'm . . . running a business'?

**Robert**    If we don't keep him in here – if we do not make this 'very costly outlay' . . .

**Bruce**    Well, it is risky.

**Robert**    How risky?

**Bruce**    *Very* risky.

**Robert**    What did he do before?

**Bruce**    Before when?

**Robert**    Before he was admitted. What happened?

**Bruce**    He was . . . he was in the market . . . doing . . . I dunno, something funny.

**Robert**    He was doing 'something funny' in the market. Which market?

**Bruce**    Does it matter?

**Robert**    I'm curious.

**Bruce**    Shepherd's Bush.

**Robert**    'Funny' strange or 'funny' ha ha?

**Bruce**   It's in the file. Read the file.

**Robert**   Why can't you just tell me?

**Bruce**   I'd rather not.

**Robert**   Why not?

**Bruce**   I'd just rather not.

*Pause.*

**Robert**   Why not?

*Pause.*

Why not, Doctor? What did he do?

**Bruce**   It's rather delicate.

**Robert**   Well, if you're going to be coy about it –

**Bruce**   I just don't think it's relevant.

**Robert**   We can't keep him in here unless he's dangerous. You know the rules.

**Bruce**   I think he's becoming depressed.

**Robert**   *I'm* becoming depressed now.

*Pause.*

Look.
Doctor. If you keep him here long enough he won't be able to go home because he won't know what home is any more. He won't know how it works any more – he won't know How To Do It. Get him out there now. Assign a community psychiatric nurse and treat him in the home – he's more comfortable, we're more comfortable, it's less of a drain on resources, the Authority is ecstatic.

**Bruce**   OK. In a perfect world, forgetting about 'resources', forgetting about 'budgetary constraints' – say we've got *unlimited beds* – what would you do?

**Robert**    In a perfect world I'd send him home with fucking bells on and spread a little happiness. Why the hell not? Now, you have a job to do. If you don't feel you can do that job, you go away and have a think for a while. You know, in the medical wilderness, in your new job proofreading for the fucking *Lancet*; writing Bolshevik columns for *Welsh Doctor Weekly*.

*Pause.*

Is he still in there? Where is he?

**Bruce**    He's in there.

**Robert**    In the . . . the . . .

**Bruce**    That little room.

**Robert**    What little room? The cleaners' room?

**Bruce**    No, the, you know. That little waiting room. That's where they go to wait. It's a new thing.

*Pause.*

**Robert**    You know, there is nothing wrong with your patient, Bruce. He may be a bit jumpy, he may be a bit brusque, a bit shouty, a bit OTT – but hey, maybe that's just what you do where he comes from.

**Bruce**    'Where he comes from'?

**Robert**    His 'community'.

**Bruce**    He comes from Shepherd's Bush. What exactly are you trying to say?

**Robert**    I'm not saying anything.

**Bruce**    'Where he comes from'? What are you saying?

**Robert**    I'm not saying anything.

**Bruce**    Go on. What are you saying?

**Robert**    Nothing.

*Pause.*

I'm only saying . . .

*Pause.*

Maybe . . . maybe, maybe it's just you. Maybe you just make him nervous. Eh?

**Bruce**   *What?*

**Robert**   Hear me out, it happens. This is the question we must ask ourselves. As a profession.

**Bruce**   'Is it me? Do I just make him nervous?'

**Robert**   Yes.

**Bruce**   He's a paranoid schizophrenic.

**Robert**   'Allegedly.'

**Bruce**   This is ridiculous.

**Robert**   We spend our lives asking whether or not this or that person is to be judged normal, a 'normal' person, a 'human', and we blithely assume that we know what 'normal' is. What 'human' is. Maybe he's more 'human' than us. Maybe *we're* the sick ones.

**Bruce**   He's 'more human than us'?

**Robert**   Yes.

**Bruce**   And we're the sick ones.

**Robert**   Maybe.

*Pause.*

**Bruce**   *Why?*

*Silence.*

**Robert**   OK, I'm being 'whimsical'. I'm being 'capricious'. But maybe, just maybe he's a *right* to be angry and paranoid and depressed and unstable. Maybe it's the only *suitable* response to the human condition.

**Bruce**    What?

**Robert**    The human species is the only species which is innately insane. 'Sanity is a conditioned response to environmental . . .

**Bruce**    I don't believe you're saying this . . .

**Robert**    . . . stimulae.' Maybe – just maybe it's true.

**Bruce**    Maybe it's *utter horseshit*. (*Beat.*) I'm sorry. Doctor Smith. But. Which, which existential novelist said that? I mean, um, you'll be quoting R. D. Laing next.

**Robert**    That was R. D. Laing.

**Bruce**    R. D. Laing was a *madman*. They don't come any fruitier.

**Robert**    I think there's something in it . . .

**Bruce**    You'll be leaping into your tights and spouting Shakespeare next: Hamlet had a Borderline Personality Disorder with Morbidity, Recklessness, Impulsiveness and a propensity for dithering.

**Robert**    He did!

**Bruce**    Should you really be telling me this? Because, when I was at med school, you know, this is not the sort of thing I learnt.

**Robert**    Well, with respect, Doctor, maybe it's time you grew up, eh? Loosen up, calm down, get your head out of your textbooks and learn a little about *humanity*. Humanity, Doctor. Being human. As the poet said, Allen Ginsberg, *Allen Ginsberg* said this, I'll never forget it . . . 'Human is not a noun, it's a *verb*.'

*Pause.*

Eh? Don't be so *old-fashioned*.

*Silence.*

**Bruce**    Allen Ginsberg.

**Robert**    OK, bad example. But listen . . .
The government guidelines clearly state that the community
is the preferred and proper place and it's our duty to
subscribe to that. Otherwise it's no end of trouble.

**Bruce**    If I let him out he will have a breakdown and
succumb to all the most horrifying symptoms of
schizophrenia undiagnosed, unchecked, unsupervised and
unmedicated.

**Robert**    Doctor Flaherty –

**Bruce**    And we can't do anything about it –

**Robert**    Doctor Flaherty.

**Bruce**    Because of policy?

**Robert**    Calm down.

**Bruce**    I'm sorry. Um, you're right. I'm calm.

**Robert**    If you detain this man any longer he will become
institutionalised.
He won't get better he'll get worse.
You will make him ill.

*Pause.*

**Bruce**    Well, um, I don't believe I will.

**Robert** *goes to the door, opens it.*

**Christopher** *comes through the door.*

**Robert**    You can come back in now. We've finished our
little chat. Sit down, there's a good fellow. Can I get you
anything, a cup of water?

**Robert** *pours another cup for* **Christopher** *who drinks thirstily.*

**Christopher** *paces a moment.*

**Bruce**    Thirsty?

**Christopher** *nods and holds his cup out for a refill. He drinks it and
goes back to pacing.*

**Bruce**    That'll be the haloperidol. Are you still stiff?

**Christopher**    I'm jumping like a leaf. I been walking it off.

**Bruce**    Try not to.

**Christopher**    I like walking.

**Bruce**    I know. And that's how you get lost.

**Christopher**    I walked to the Hanger Lane Gyratory once.

**Bruce**    I know. I'm sure it was wonderful.

**Robert**    Bravo.

**Bruce**    No, not Bravo, you must try and control it.

**Robert**    Oh, let him walk if he wants to walk. Goodness gracious. You go ahead and walk to Hanger Lane. Enjoy. Now. When were you planning on leaving us?

**Christopher** (*pacing*)    Twenty-four hours.

**Robert**    Morning, evening?

**Christopher**    After I had my lunch.

**Robert**    And you have somewhere to go I take it.

**Bruce**    Council accommodation. White City.

**Robert**    Marvellous.

**Christopher**    Only I don't go there.

**Robert**    Oh.

**Christopher**    I don't like White City.

**Robert**    Why not?

**Christopher**    Cos of the Fuzz.

**Robert**    The 'Fuzz'.

**Christopher**    The Filth. The Pigs. The Cops. The 'Old Bill'.

**Robert**   The police?

**Christopher**   I get stopped a *lot* in White City.
That's why I was arrested in Shepherd's Bush. Cos they all
talk to each other on their walkie-talkies. They was waiting
for me. They came to get me in the market. Come all the way
from White City for me. Believe. I lost my shit.

**Robert**   I see, well –

**Christopher**   Cos they was after me, man.

**Robert**   And why do you think that is?

**Christopher**   What? *Why*?

**Robert**   Yes, why? Why were they 'after you'?

**Christopher**   Why do you *think*, man?

**Robert**   I'm asking you.

**Christopher**   Cos they're *fascists*. It's obvious.

*Silence.*

**Robert**   Where would you like to live?

**Christopher**   Where?

**Robert**   Would you prefer?

**Christopher**   Africa.

**Robert**   Africa.

*Pause.*

**Christopher** *sits and stares at* **Robert** *with intensity.*

**Robert**   Aha ha ha. Yes, very good. And why not?

**Christopher**   I already told you.

**Robert**   Yes, but I mean, for the time being.

**Christopher**   There is no time being. I'm going to Africa.
Central Africa. Where my dad come from.

**Robert**    Ah. Well . . . when you get out, if you, if things work out for you and you get a . . . have you got a job to go back to?

**Christopher**    Got a job in Africa.

**Robert**    O . . . K . . . Somewhere to stay?

**Christopher**    In Africa. In Uganda.

*Silence.*

**Robert**    Friends?

**Christopher**    In Africa.

**Robert** (*beat*)    Excellent.

**Robert** *stands.*

*He hands the notes back to* **Bruce**.

**Robert**    Well, I think I've pretty much finished here. Doctor Flaherty?

**Bruce**    You're finished?

**Robert**    Quite finished. It's been nice chatting to you, Christopher. I sincerely hope I never clap eyes on you again, e-heh heh heh.

*He shakes* **Christopher**'s *hand and* **Christopher** *just stares at him.*

**Robert**    It's a joke.

**Bruce**    So you're just going now?

**Robert**    Is that a problem? Unless you want me for anything else?

*They all look at each other.*

**Christopher** *is still holding* **Robert**'s *hand.*

**Christopher** (*to* **Robert**)    What's up with him? (*To* **Bruce**.) What's up your arse, man?

**Bruce**   If you don't mind, I'd like you to stay while I ask Chris a couple more questions.

**Robert**   What sort of questions?

**Bruce**   Routine. My assessment isn't over yet.

**Robert** *sits reluctantly, taking his hand back.*

**Robert**   Why not? Fire away.

**Bruce**   Because, the thing is, Chris, Doctor Smith here says that you can go if you want to.

**Christopher**   I know. I'm going.

**Bruce**   But I'm wondering if you really want to?

**Christopher**   I want it *bad*, d'you know what I mean?

**Bruce**   And . . . you're *sure* you're ready. Are you sure?

**Christopher**   I'm cool.

*Pause.*

**Bruce**   OK. Just a couple of questions.

**Christopher**   Shoot.

**Bruce**   What's in the fruit bowl?

**Christopher**   How d'you mean?

**Bruce**   What do you see in the fruit bowl? What type of fruit do you see?

*He proffers the bowl full of oranges.* **Christopher** *stares at it long and hard.* **Bruce** *takes an orange from the bowl and hands it to* **Christopher** *who stares at it hard.*

*He also tosses one to* **Robert**.

**Bruce**   What's in the bowl, Chris?

**Christopher**   Oranges.

**Bruce**   Oranges, good, but what sort of oranges?

**Christopher**    Just oranges.

**Bruce**    Yes, but they're not *orange* oranges, are they?

**Christopher**    Nope.

**Bruce**    What did you tell me yesterday? Can you remember?

*Pause.*

**Christopher**    They're blue oranges.

**Bruce**    Blue oranges. Really?

**Christopher**    Bright blue.

**Bruce**    Peel one. See what's inside.

*They wait as* **Christopher** *peels the orange, holds it up.*

**Bruce**    What colour is it inside?

*Pause.*

Chris?

**Christopher**    It's blue.

**Bruce**    So the skin is blue – and even underneath the skin it's the same – it's blue?

**Christopher**    That's correct. Completely blue.

*Pause.*

It's bad. It's a bad orange. Don't eat it.

*Pause.*

I mean, my God! Ha ha. What is it? 'Black magic'?

**Bruce**    Voodoo.

**Christopher**    Voodoo! Oh no. *Spooky.* D'you know what I mean? It's – it's – it's *nuts.*

**Bruce**    'Spooky'.

**Christopher**    Spooky. 'Yikes!'

**Bruce**    'Yikes' indeed . . .

**Christopher**    'This bad nigga dude we got doing his voodoo again.'

*Pause.*

My dad, right, my dad, that's his favourite fruit. Oranges. *Orange* oranges, though. D'you know what I mean?

**Bruce**    Who is your father, Chris? Chris?

*Pause.*

**Christopher** *eats a segment of orange.*

**Bruce**    Who is your father?

**Christopher**    How d'you mean?

**Bruce**    What's his name?

**Christopher**    I already told you.

**Bruce**    Tell me again. In front of Robert.

**Christopher**    Why?

**Bruce**    Just . . . please, Chris . . . it's a simple question.

**Christopher**    It's difficult to answer. D'you know what I mean?

**Bruce**    No I don't. Why?

**Christopher**    If I ask you who your father is nobody gives a shit. With me it's front-page news. D'you understand?

**Bruce**    No, I don't understand. Why is it front-page news?

**Christopher**    Cos of who he is.

**Robert**    Who is he?

**Christopher**    I'm not telling you.

**Bruce**    (This is ridiculous.) Look. Please. Help me out here.

**Christopher**    You want *me* to help *you*? Now you want me to do your job.

**Robert**    If you can't tell us who he is – it'll be tricky for us to send you home. You will have to stay here. Do you understand?

**Bruce**    Who's your father, Chris?

*Pause.*

**Christopher**    It sounds silly.

**Bruce**    For Christ's sake –

**Christopher**    It's embarrassing.

**Bruce**    Chris!

**Christopher**    How can I say it, in all honesty, without you thinking I'm off the stick? How do I know it won't incriminate me, d'you know what I'm saying?

**Robert**    It won't incriminate you. We promise.

**Christopher**    Oh you 'promise'? Well, in that case, I feel a whole lot better.

**Bruce**    Please . . . just do this one thing for me. For me.

*Pause.*

**Christopher**    My father . . . my dad . . . was a very important man.

*Pause.*

Believe it or not . . . my dad . . . is former Ugandan President His Excellency Idi Amin.

**Bruce**    Fabulous –

**Christopher**    And if he knew where I was now I would not want to be you.

**Bruce**    Y – Chris –

**Christopher**    I would not want to be you.
Because The Man Does Not Fuck About, d'you understand
what I'm saying?
He will *digest* you.
He will juice you and squirt you out of his arse like a
motherfucking firehose, into the sewers for the bats and the
fish.
They don't call him 'The Butcher of the Bush' for nothing.
Believe.

*Silence.*

**Robert**    Fine . . . OK . . .

**Christopher**    What else d'you want to know?

**Robert**    Well –

**Christopher**    He got forty-three children and a hundred
grandchildren. He's a family man. He's a Muslim. He lives in
Saudi Arabia. In exile. 'Cept when he goes on holiday to
Paris. Every day he takes a delivery of East African oranges
from the airport. Reminds him of old times.
He drives a Chevrolet and has a talent for the accordion. A
lot of exiles drive Mercedes but he don't like to draw
attention to his self.

**Robert**    I see . . .

**Christopher**    He kicked my mum out of Uganda cos she's
from Zaire. He kicked out all the foreigners. D'you know
what I mean? I'm not proud of it. It's just the way he was.
Old-fashioned.

*Pause.*

**Robert**    'Old . . . fashioned'. Mm . . .

*Pause.*

Your mother is from Zaire, you say?

**Christopher**    You don't believe me, do you?

**Robert**    When was this?

**Christopher**    1974. Before I was born.

**Robert**    *Before* you were born?

**Christopher**    I was *conceived*. That's why she had to go. He couldn't father a foreigner. It's obvious.

**Bruce** *and* **Robert** *stare at each other.*

**Christopher**    He's got another wife in Haringey who runs a chippy. Got closed down for bad hygiene, d'you know what I mean?

**Bruce**    You can go back to your ward now. Chris? I'll see you later.

**Christopher**    But –

**Bruce**    It's over now.

**Christopher**    We finished?

**Bruce**    We're finished for today, yes.

**Christopher**    What did I say?

**Robert**    Absolutely nothing.

**Christopher**    Did I pass?

**Bruce** *just smiles.*

**Christopher**    Now you're not saying anything. That's no good.

**Bruce**    You have nothing to worry about.

**Christopher**    I don't, yeah?

**Bruce**    No. You're going to be fine.

**Christopher**    I'm still going home, right?

*Pause.*

I'm still going home, yeah?

*Pause.*

I'm . . . I'm still going home?

**Robert**   Shhhh . . . OK? Just relax.

*Pause.*

**Christopher**   But . . . I'm –

**Robert**   Shhh.

*Pause.*

**Christopher**   I'm –

**Robert** (*waving a finger*)   Uh. Uh-uh.

*Pause.*

**Christopher**   But I'm still going home, aren't I?

**Robert**   Of course you are.

**Bruce**   Chris? I'll speak to you later. Go back to your ward now.

**Christopher**   But I'm still going home, yeah?

**Robert**   Yes.

**Bruce** *takes back the remains of the orange,* **Christopher** *gets up and shuffles out.*

**Robert** *takes the remains of the orange from* **Bruce** *and eats a segment.*

**Robert**   Very interesting.

**Bruce**   Happy?

**Robert**   'Le Monde est Bleu comme une Orange'.

**Bruce**   What?

**Robert**   It's a poem by Paul Éluard. He was a French surrealist.

**Bruce**   You don't say.

**Robert**   'The World is as Blue as an Orange'. (*Beat.*) It's an analogy.

**Bruce**   Classic hallucinatory behaviour.

**Robert**   Or is it a simile?

**Bruce**   Already he's building a system of logic around it . . . his '*father*' who loves oranges de da de da de da.

**Robert**   Hypomania. Brief psychotic episode requiring short-term hospital treatment and a course of antipsychotics when he goes home. Simple.

**Bruce**   What if it isn't? What if it's just the tip of the iceberg?

**Robert**   Is he hearing voices? Auditory hallucinations?

**Bruce**   Not yet.

**Robert**   Is he seeing things – other than blue oranges?

**Bruce**   Isn't this enough?

**Robert** (*shrugs*)   For some reason he wants to see blue instead of orange. Neurotics do it all the time. They see what they want to see, not what they really see. Maybe he knows the poem.

**Bruce**   You're joking, aren't you?

**Robert**   Entirely serious. There's a lot of French speakers in Central Africa. His mother could have read it him as a child. It planted an image in his mind. When he's not a hundred per cent that image presents itself.

**Bruce**   You are joking.

**Robert**   There's a Tintin book. *Tintin and the Blue Oranges*. It's about a 'mad professor' who invents an orange which will grow in the Sahara. Only trouble is it's bright blue and tastes salty. Tintin was banned in the Belgian Congo. They thought he was a communist. But in colonial Uganda the notoriety no doubt made Tintin a 'must read' for the bourgeoisie. He was

a cultural icon and a symbol of middle-class insurrection. A delusion waiting to happen.
BPD with Delusion.

**Bruce**    Are you making this up?

**Robert** *shakes his head.*

**Bruce**    Surely, you must agree, there's something terribly wrong here. Surely we have a responsibility to . . .

**Robert**    A responsibility to let him out. Level 2. Prescribe medication, CPN twice weekly.

**Bruce**    He won't take medication, you know that, they never do.

**Robert**    That's what we have CPNs for. Just till he's back on his feet.

**Bruce**    He needs looking after.

**Robert**    Maybe he does, maybe he doesn't.
Maybe he really does have some connection with Idi Amin. Jesus Christ-on-a-mountain-bike. The man was spawning offspring all over the shop.

**Bruce**    You can't be serious.

**Robert**    Maybe I am.

**Bruce**    Oh for God's sake.

**Robert**    OK, calm down.

*He paces and wipes his hands on his shirt, rubs his hands together, talks with a mouthful.*

Now (*clears his throat*) for what it's worth, it's quite possible he's heard some family story, handed down through the generations, some apocryphal story, maybe Idi Amin came to town, to the village, de da de da de da, Chinese whispers, it's just gathered importance, gained in stature and now he believes this. It happens. Read my manuscript.

**Bruce**    What manuscript?

**Robert**    It's a continuation of my PhD really. It's not finished. There's a chapter missing – something rather complex and enigmatic – a certain *je ne sais quoi* although I can't think what.
Seriously. I think there's something in it.

**Bruce**    I think there's something in feng shui, Doctor, but I wouldn't do a PhD in it.

**Robert**    As your supervisor I wouldn't have it any other way.

**Bruce**    I read your PhD. 'Cultural Antecedent and Cultural Specificity in Connection with a Delusional Belief System'. Enables us to understand the origins of delusion. African tribesmen develop delusions about sorcerers; Westerners develop delusions about the Spice Girls and extraterrestrials. The specifics of Christopher's cultural background are that his mother once lived in Uganda: he's got a delusion about a Ugandan dictator she no doubt talked about. You're saying he's not sick, it's a cultural thing.

**Robert**    I'm saying he's not mad. There's a difference.

*Pause.*

Do you know what happened to his mother in Uganda? Do you know whether she was raped by soldiers after the military coup? By Idi Amin himself? She could have been a journalist or a cook at State House for all you know. Have you asked her?

**Bruce**    That's not possible.

**Robert**    Why not?

**Bruce**    I can't trace her. We think she lives in Feltham.

**Robert**    Where in Feltham?

**Bruce**    Nobody seems to have an address.

**Robert**    Find her. It might not all be true – but then again it might.

Can you imagine the ramifications of that?
This is precisely what I'm getting at in my research.

**Bruce**   What are you talking about? You can't use him for research.

**Robert**   Why not? Why ever not? Think about it.
There is more mental illness amongst the Afro-Caribbean population in London than any other ethnic grouping.
Why?
Is it the way we're diagnosing it? Is it us? Is it them? What's causing it? What's the answer? What's the cure?
There's no 'cure' for schizophrenia.
No 'cure' for psychosis.
Only *palliative drugs*.
But what if it *isn't* psychosis? Wouldn't that be a relief? What if there is a cure? *Cognitive* therapy. *Minimal* medication.
A 'cure' for 'black psychosis'.
Imagine it.
The Holy Grail.
And imagine if the fucker who found it was . . . us.

*Silence.*

**Bruce**   'A Cure for Black Psychosis'.

**Robert**   Figuratively speaking.

**Bruce**   You're being 'whimsical' again?

**Robert** (*shaking his head*)   An end to palliatives. No more 'dated toxic crud'.

**Bruce**   OK. Say it is true. It's all true. Christopher is Idi Amin's son. And he's schizophrenic. It's both. Had you thought of that?

*Pause.*

Kind of blows your theory out of the water, doesn't it?

*Silence.*

**Robert**    OK, look. I'm merely pointing out that sometimes
our analysis is *ethnocentric*: in this case you are evaluating the
situation according to your own specific cultural criteria.

**Bruce**    'Ethnocentric'?

**Robert**    Our colonial antecedents are latent and barely
suppressed. We are intuitively suspicious because of our
cultural background.
For example, on the way back from the rugby the other night
we stopped at the off-licence for a bottle of wine. I noticed
that the Pakistani gentleman behind the counter said neither
Please nor Thank you. I had to ask myself, is he just *like*
that – is he just *rude*? Or is it because there is no such thing as
Please and Thank you in Urdu – is it not customary in his
culture?

**Bruce**    What are you talking about? He always says Please
and Thank you.

**Robert**    OK, fine. So perhaps I should ask myself, Is it me?
What are *my* cultural expectations?

**Bruce**    Look, after the rugby, everybody goes in there, all
the rugger buggers, pissy drunk and *they* don't say Please and
Thank you –

**Robert**    Nevertheless, we must guard against our
ethnocentricity.

**Bruce**    I don't think I like the direction this is heading.

**Robert**    The point is, this is my *province*, Doctor.
That's why you asked me here.
Because I know how many beans make five.
I am, as they say, an 'expert'.
I am Senior Consultant and I am here to be 'consulted'.
I am not here to be 'bounced off'.
To 'run it up the flag pole and see who salutes'.
I'm here because 'I know'.

**Bruce**    But . . . with the greatest respect, Doctor Smith, you
don't. He's *my* patient . . . so . . . really . . .

**Robert**   OK, fine. Whatever. Discharge him. Next case.

*Pause.*

**Bruce**   But –

**Robert**   We can skin this cat as artfully as we like.
However, in the opinion of this highly experienced
Department Head, Doctor Flaherty, what we have here is No
Beds and, more importantly, a patient who has No Need of a
Bed.

**Bruce**   But I think –

**Robert**   What I 'think' is that you think too much.
What I think is that you should let me do the thinking.
Now if you don't mind, I'm very busy.

**Robert** *goes to the door.*

**Bruce**   But . . . you're saying . . . what you're really saying
is Christopher's . . . unable to distinguish between realistic
and utterly unrealistic notions because . . . what . . . ? Because
he's . . . ?

**Robert**   BPD. Case closed.

**Bruce**   It's because he's b –

**Robert**   BPD. Goodbye, Doctor.

**Bruce**   Because he's black?

**Robert** *sighs, clenches his teeth. Walks back into the room.*

**Robert** (*icily*)   I'm saying where he comes from it is almost
certainly not an unrealistic notion. Where we come from, it
evidently is. Get it?

**Bruce**   But he comes from Shepherd's Bush.

**Robert**   He sees himself as African. And we don't say
'black' any more –

**Bruce**   Yes we do –

**Robert**   We say 'Afro-Caribbean'.

**Bruce**    Where does the Caribbean come into it?

**Robert**    All right, he's 'African'.

**Bruce**    From Shepherd's Bush.

**Robert**    I'm not going to quibble over this twaddle.

**Bruce**    'Twaddle'?

**Robert**    I'm not going to squabble. His 'origins' are in Africa.

**Bruce**    How far back are you going?

**Robert**    And for the last time I'll remind you that you are under my supervision, you are my subordinate, and your tone is beginning to sound dangerously insubordinate if not nakedly insulting.

**Bruce**    I'm sorry . . . but –

**Robert**    Do you know what most young doctors would do to have me as Supervisor? I mean, normal ones . . . the smart ones . . . what they'd do to know they have a future. To have a shot at becoming Consultant? They'd *lick my anus*.

*Silence.*

(But that's beside the point . . .)

*He goes to the door and looks out.*
*Comes back. Sits.*

Now. Do you want me to recommend your consultancy at this hospital or don't you?

**Bruce**    Of course.

**Robert**    Then act like a professional. Act like a representative of the Royal College of Psychiatrists.

**Bruce**    But I'm *not* a –

**Robert**    Do you want to be? Mm? Now. Pull yourself together. Try not to be so wet behind the ears. Otherwise I'm taking you off this case.

**Bruce**    You can't take me off this case.

**Robert**    I'll assign a CPN and discharge him myself.

**Bruce**    If you do I'll appeal to the Authority.

**Robert**    I am the Authority. (Just between you and me.)

**Bruce**    But . . . um . . . with respect, it's it's it's it's what I believe in.

**Robert**    Well, you know, Doctor, with respect, that isn't good enough.

**Bruce**    It's not good enough that I do what I believe is right?

**Robert**    That's right. It's naive.

**Bruce**    *Naive?*

**Robert**    That's right. You're naive. And you're beginning to get on my *wick*.

*Silence.*

**Bruce**    Why won't you listen to me?

**Robert**    What? 'Listen to you'? To you? It's not my job to listen to you. It's your job to . . . oh for goodness' sake . . .

*Pause.*

OK. All right. Listen.
Let me join up some of the dots for you.
Let me do some of the maths for you:
Schizophrenia is the worst pariah.
One of the last great taboos.
People don't understand it.
They don't want to understand it.
It scares them.
It depresses them.
It is not treatable with glamorous and intriguing wonderdrugs like Prozac or Viagra.
It isn't newsworthy.

It isn't curable.
It isn't heroin or Ecstasy.
It is not the preserve of rock stars and supermodels and hip
young authors.
It is not a topic of dinner-party conversation.
*Organised crime* gets better press.
They make *movies* about junkies and alcoholics and gangsters
and men who drink too much, fall over and beat their woman
until bubbles come out of her nose, but schizophrenia, my
friend, is just not in the phone book.

**Bruce**    Then we must change that.

**Robert**    . . . And they . . . *what*?

**Bruce**    Then we must change that.

**Robert**    'Change'. Hmm. Well . . . the thing is, you can't
change that. D'you see? I can't. Seriously.
The Authority – the rest of the Board, not even me – they will
question your expertise. They will wonder why you got so
upset about it. They will wonder whether or not this case has
a 'deeper personal significance' to you and they will
undermine you at every turn and then they will screw you. As
sure as eggs are fucking eggs.

**Bruce**    A 'deeper personal . . .'?

**Robert**    People will question your mental *wellness*.

*Silence.*

They'll say you're mad.
And then they'll say *I'm* mad for supervising you and allowing
my department to disintegrate so.

**Bruce**    Well, if you don't want to supervise me . . . if you've
changed your mind . . . you only have to say.

**Robert**    Not at all. This is a 'Teaching Hospital' and I am
here to teach.

**Bruce**    W . . . was it Saturday? Did I say something after
the rugby?

**Robert**   Look. I'm not the big bad wolf. I'm not trying to undermine your decision and I certainly don't want to release Christopher if he isn't ready. I *care*. And I know you care. All I'm saying is sometimes one can care *too much*. One can have too much Empathy – Understanding – an *overweening* Compassion. You try to be all things to all men: Doctor. Friend. A *reasonable* man. We all want to be *reasonable* men. Eh? Bruce? Please. Now. Am I not your friend?

*Pause.*

Aren't we friends?

**Bruce** *slowly nods.*

**Robert**   Sleep on it.
Let me conduct my own assessment. We can reconvene in the morning and all decide together. Eh? I'll talk to him tonight. I promise you I won't be partisan.

**Bruce**   OK. Fine. Whatever you say.

**Robert**   Don't look so gloomy. Just wait till you're a consultant. Think of that loft conversion.

**Bruce**   Robert . . .

**Robert**   Bruce . . . Bruce . . . Bruce . . .
You have it all to look forward to.
Trust me.
I want what you want. I really do.
I believe in what you believe in.
I'm On Your Side.

*Blackout.*

# Act Two

*That night.* **Robert** *and* **Christopher** *sit facing each other across the table. A reading light is the only light.*

**Robert** *takes a cigarette from his pack and lights it.* **Christopher** *takes a cigarette from behind his ear and* **Robert** *lights it. They exhale.*

**Robert**   Listen listen listen listen.

*Pause.*

Listen.

*Pause.*

We all have these thoughts. It's perfectly natural. Even I have them. Yes. Me. Some days I get home from work, from a long night in the hospital, visiting, ward rounds, nothing untoward, nothing terrible, a few cross words with a colleague, some silly argument, I get home and I get in the door and I *slump*. All the life drains out of me. I think . . . Why Am I Doing This? Eh? What's in it for me? A table at the Ivy if I use the right prefix. A seminar in Norway. Some spotty young registrar takes me to the rugby and hangs on my every word. Big deal. And there are times, when I look across at this professor and that professor turning up to work in a new *Jag*, he's just come back from La Rochelle, he's off to play a round of golf at his thousand-pound-a-year golf club, have a drink at his jolly old Mayfair club, posh dinners with drug company reps, knighthoods, appearances on Radio Four n'ha ha ha . . .
And I think . . . How do they do that?
What, are they 'experts' or something?
I Want To Be Professor!
What do they do that I don't?
And the answer is:
Who *cares*? That's *their* life. Nevertheless, I feel small and I think my life adds up to nothing. And I have to keep reminding myself: Why not? Why not think these things? It's

not greedy, it's not covetous. It's *human*. It's me being a human being. And it applies to us all. And it's my right to do something about it. It's everybody's right to take steps.
But *killing yourself*?
Christopher?
Why?

*Silence.*

Everybody Feels Like This. At some point. In their life. Everybody feels that they've . . . lost out. It's the Human Condition. The capacity to feel *disappointment*. It's what distinguishes us from the animals. Our *disappointment*. Mm. It's true. The capacity to grieve for lost opportunity. For the lives we *could* have *led*. The men or women we *may* have become. It has us in an appalling stranglehold.
And sometimes we say, Why Go On? And we want to end it all. The hell with it. Life's a sham.
*That's* human too. You don't hear doggies running about going, 'Oh that this too too solid flesh would melt.' Of course not. Why not? They're *dogs*! It would be ridiculous. Dogs have other talents. They can lick their own balls. A talent for simplicity. N'ha ha ha. Do you see? Learn to cultivate a Talent for Simplicity.

*Pause.*

**Christopher**   Learn to Lick My Balls?
That's your expert advice, yeah?

**Robert**   N'ha ha ha. N'ha ha ha, well . . . it might work . . .

**Christopher**   You're a fucking *doctor*, man.

**Robert**   I know, I'm joking, but you, you, you see my point. This life is a *gift*. The food we eat, the smells we smell, the trees, the sky, the *fecundity* of Creation . . . It's a *really lovely* gift, and if for whatever reason you cannot see that right now, then I'm here to Heal Your Vision. To help you. See. I promise you, I plead with you, I *entreat* you. Take a few deep breaths. Calm down. Think about this. You're not 'suicidal'. It's ridiculous.

*Silence.*

**Christopher**    I don't want to go home.

*Pause.*

I changed my mind. I'm not going.

**Robert**    Christopher . . .

**Christopher**    I . . . I . . . I don't have a home. I'm not . . .
I'm not ready.

**Robert**    What happens to you when you go home?

**Christopher**    I told you about the Fuzz.

**Robert**    OK. Fine. But apart from . . . the 'Fuzz'. What else
happens to you?

*Pause.*

Chris?

*Pause.*

**Christopher**    People stare at me. Like they know . . . like
they know about me.
Like they know something about me that I don't know.

**Robert**    Such as?

**Christopher**    Eh?

**Robert**    What could they know that you don't know?

**Christopher**    I don't know. They hate me. They think
I'm bad.

**Robert**    Which people?

**Christopher**    Eh?

**Robert**    Who are these people who . . . think you're bad?

**Christopher**    I hear noises. At night. Outside my window.
Sometimes I hear . . . talking. People talking about me.

**Robert**    Talking about you?

**Christopher**    Laughing sometimes.

**Robert**    And you've no idea who it is?

**Christopher**    No idea. Sometimes I hear machinery. Whirring. Like a . . . a strange droning noise. And beeping. A strange beeping noise. Very loud.

**Robert**    It's the dustbin men.

**Christopher**    On Saturdays and Sundays?

**Robert**    Builders. OK? We're in the midst of a property boom. Interest rates are low, people are buying and building and renovating – people want more of the life gifted them. Life is Rich. People are greedy for Life.

**Christopher**    Not in White City they're not. 'White City'. 'South Africa Road'. Even the names are a fucking wind-up.

**Robert**    But you have your friends. Your *community*. People who care.

**Christopher**    I don't have any friends.
I try to make friends with people but it's not easy. I try to make conversation but it's not easy. Sometimes I say the wrong thing.
Actually I always say the wrong thing. I don't have a girlfriend. Who'd want me?

*Pause.*

**Robert**    Well. You'll make new friends when you get out.

**Christopher**    I made friends with Bruce.

**Robert**    You won't be alone in all this. I'll make sure of that.

**Christopher**    Yeah but I want double glazing. Don't talk to me about the fucking property boom. It's like living in a biscuit tin.

*Pause.*

**Robert**   Well, you know, Chris, I can't provide you with double glazing. It's not part of my remit. If you want double glazing . . .
Go to the Council. See your housing officer.

**Christopher**   You said you would help me.

**Robert**   I know, but –

**Christopher**   So help me –

**Robert**   It's –

**Christopher**   Help me –

**Robert**   It's not my job! N'ha ha ha. D'you see?

**Christopher**   Yeah, but what I thought was, if I moved somewhere else –

**Robert**   OK. There's a procedure for that. The Council will have a procedure for transferring you.

**Christopher**   Yeah, but I wanna go to Africa.

**Robert**   You want to go to Africa.

**Christopher**   I want to go to Africa.

**Robert**   Back to your roots.

**Christopher**   My 'roots'?

**Robert**   You feel you 'belong' there?

**Christopher**   *No*, man. I already told you. It's nice there. And and and you know I told you about my dad.

**Robert**   Idi Amin.

**Christopher**   Idi Amin Dada. That's his proper name. Idi Amin Dada.

**Robert**   O . . . K . . .

*Pause.*

Tell me about your mother. What did she do in Uganda?

**Christopher**   She was a barmaid.

**Robert**   A 'barmaid'. Really? In a pub?

**Christopher**   No, in a shoe shop, innit.

**Robert**   Where the soldiers drank?

**Christopher**   Eh?

**Robert**   Did many soldiers drink there?

**Christopher**   I don't know.

**Robert**   What I'm getting at is . . . how . . . how did your mum actually meet President Amin?

*Silence.*

**Christopher** *stares into space.*

**Robert**   Christopher?

**Christopher**   You wouldn't understand.

**Robert**   Why wouldn't I understand?

**Christopher**   You wouldn't understand.

*Silence.*

**Robert**   Try me.

**Christopher**   She was a student. He closed down the university for political reasons.

**Robert**   She told you this?

**Christopher**   She never talks about it – d'you know what I mean? It's personal.

*Pause.*

She gets upset.

**Robert**   What did she read?

**Christopher**   How d'you mean?

**Robert**   What was her subject? English literature?

**Christopher**    How d'you mean?

**Robert**    What I'm getting at is, well, does she read you poetry, for example? Or plays?

**Christopher**    No.

**Robert**    What about at school? Did you read poetry at school?

**Christopher**    No.

**Robert**    Oh. OK. Fine.

*Pause.*

What about books? Children's books? Comics? *Tintin*? *Asterix*? She must have given you books.

**Christopher**    No.

**Robert**    Do you still see her? Christopher? D'you know where she lives?

*Pause.*

Chris?

**Christopher**    She lives in Feltham.

**Robert**    Do you know her address? Do you want to tell me?

*Pause.*

You don't want to tell me where she lives?
Why should I believe you if you can't even tell me your mother's address?

**Christopher**    Bruce don't believe me either but I can prove it.

**Robert**    You can 'prove it'?

**Christopher**    Yeah, man.

**Robert**    How?

**Christopher**    Why should I tell you?

**Robert**    Well . . . because I'm asking you to . . .

**Christopher**    What if I don't trust you?

**Robert**    Well . . . then . . . that would be a great shame.

**Christopher**    A shame? (*Beat.*) You think it'd be a shame,
yeah?

**Robert**    Yeah.

**Christopher**    Oh.

**Christopher** *weighs it up.*
*He produces a wallet from his pocket.*
*From the wallet he produces a tightly folded-up newspaper article.*
*He unfolds it and holds it out to* **Robert**.
**Robert** *hesitates, then takes it and reads.*
**Christopher** *reads over his shoulder.*

**Robert** (*reading*)    'A delivery of East African oranges from
the airport . . . the Butcher of the Bush . . . talent for the
accordion blah blah blah . . . Forty-three children by four
wives . . .'

**Christopher**    Five wives.

**Robert**    Eh?

**Christopher**    Five wives really. There's a fifth. A secret one.

**Robert**    A . . . a . . . where?

**Christopher** (*pointing*)    Not the one who runs a chippy.
Another one. Common-law wife. Living in 'penury'.

**Robert** (*reading*)    'Living in . . . in Feltham.'

**Christopher**    In 'penury'.

**Robert**    'In penury . . . in Feltham.' Bugger me. How long
have you had this?

**Christopher**    My mother gave it to me.

**Robert**    Bugger me.

*They look at each other.*

*Silence.*

**Robert** *puts his fingertips to his temples momentarily, thinking hard.*

**Christopher** (*pointing*)    Look. That's his photo.

**Robert** (*holding the article*)    Can I keep this?

**Christopher**    No you cannot keep that.

**Robert**    Please. Christopher . . . listen . . .

**Christopher** *snatches the article back, folds it, puts it away as he speaks.*

**Christopher**    I am being *harassed.* I'm in fear of my *life.* I live in *fear.* They Know Who I Am.

**Robert**    Who does?

**Christopher**    The men. Where I live. The noises. The . . . the police. It all makes sense.

**Robert**    They're . . . look . . . it's . . . they're just ordinary *men. Work* men . . . *police* men.

**Christopher**    Other men too. Another man. He throws bananas at me.

**Robert**    Bananas . . . ?

**Christopher**    When I'm at work. Even at work – d'you know what I mean! Big bloke with a little pointy head. Long thin arms trailing along the ground. A real knuckle-dragger. Very white skin. Hideous-looking bastard. He's the ring-leader. I see him at night. He bangs on my door. Says he's coming to get me. He says he'll do me and nobody would even notice and I believe him. There's a whole family of them. A tribe. I don't like them at all. They're a race apart. *Zombies!* The undead. Monsters!
QPR supporters.

*Pause.*

**Robert**   Football hooligans?

**Christopher**   On Saturdays, I seem 'em in the crowds at
Loftus Road.
They come after the game. And before the game. With
bananas.
With . . . with shit smeared through the letter box, not dog
shit – real shit. Pissing through the letter box, fires,
firestarting on the front step. It's a disgrace. They call me
'Jungle Boy'. If my dad was here he'd kill them dead.
He'd monster them.
Believe.

*Silence.*

It's their appearance that spooks me the most. Those tiny,
bony, shrunken heads. All shaved. Ugly.

**Robert**   D'you mean . . . Skinheads?

**Christopher**   *Zombies.*

**Robert**   What makes you think these people are . . . 'the
undead'?

**Christopher**   They look *half* dead. It's that ghostly white
skin, looks like tapioca, d'you know what I mean?

**Robert**   Christopher –

**Christopher**   Baldies. 'Baldy-Heads', that's what I call
them. Baldy-Heads.

**Robert**   'Baldy-Heads'. I see. But . . . they're not really . . .
'Zombies', now are they? Chris? Which is it, 'Zombies' or
'Baldy-Heads'?

*Pause.*

There is a difference.

**Christopher**   D'you think it's funny?

**Robert**   Not in the least. It could be the difference between
you staying here or you going home.

**Christopher**    They're *dangerous*, man. Believe. They're spooky. I could be dead tomorrow.

**Robert** *rubs his eyes and sighs.*

**Christopher**    You know the average life expectancy of the modern black male? Sixty-four years old. That's how long we got. What age do we get the pension? *Sixty-five!* It's a fucking *rip-off*, man! D'you know what I mean?

**Robert**    So . . . fundamentally, you don't think you're sick? Am I right?

**Christopher**    Yeah I'm sick. Sick and tired, man. Sick of everything. I got problems. D'you know what I'm saying?

**Robert**    Do you keep a diary?

**Christopher**    A diary? No. Do you?

**Robert**    You should start keeping a diary.

**Christopher**    I never go out.

**Robert**    No, a diary of what *happens*.

**Christopher**    Nothing ever happens, man. All day every day, nothing.

**Robert**    I meant, things on the estate. Concerning the letter box . . . ? OK?
Then you go to the Council, you ask to see your housing officer and you show her the diary. She can have you transferred to a different estate.

**Christopher**    It gets a bit lonely sometimes but –

**Robert**    Yes I know and that's OK. That's normal. That's human. And I'll tell you something else –

**Christopher**    Sometimes people scare me.

**Robert**    I know they do. And you know what you do when they do these things?

**Christopher**    What?

**Robert**    You laugh.

**Christopher**    Laugh?

**Robert**    When somebody hurts you, just laugh at them.
You don't care. They'll soon get the message.

*Pause.*

**Christopher**    Laugh, yeah?

**Robert**    It drives them crazy. Really, it's a good trick.

**Christopher**    Oh I get you. Laugh. Really.
HA HA HA HA HA. HA HA HA HA HA. 'Laugh and the
whole world laughs with you.'
AND THEN THEY LOCK YOU UP!
What the fuck are you on about, man? D'you know what I
mean? Pull yourself together!

**Robert**    OK. Cry. Do handstands. Express Yourself. Just
Don't Take It Personally.

**Christopher**    'Express myself'. And who are you:
'Professor Groovy'?

**Robert**    Strictly speaking it's 'Doctor Groovy'. N'ha ha ha
ha. N'ha ha ha. See? You can do it.

*Silence.*

No. You're quite right. I'm sorry. But, you see, the thing is,
Chris, I don't think that you are ill and I want you to try to
settle down somewhere.

**Christopher**    What I'm saying is, Doctor, I been unlucky
where I been housed, yeah?

**Robert**    Well then . . . you need to be rehoused not locked up.

**Christopher**    I get scared out there.

**Robert**    I know, I know. And, look, I'll let you into a secret.
Are you listening? I get scared too.

**Christopher**     What are you scared of?

**Robert**     Eh?

**Christopher**     What are you scared of?

**Robert**     Everything. My life. Academia.

*Pause.*

I'm lonely too. Everybody –

**Christopher**     Why are you lonely?

**Robert**     Supposing I don't measure up.
Supposing my research is less well received than anticipated and then I have no friends.
Supposing I never make Professor.
Supposing nobody wants to hear my ideas.
Nobody wants to talk to me.
And and and even when they *do* talk to me, is it the real *me* they're talking to? Or is it Somebody Up There in the . . .
Academic Firmament. Some Great Illustrious Thinker.
Mister Big Cheese Head of Department. Somebody I'm Just Not. You see?

*Pause.*

Everybody's scared. Everybody's lonely.

**Christopher**     I think Bruce is right. I'm not ready. I don't wanna go.

**Robert**     OK . . . well . . . did he actually say that to you, did he?

**Christopher**     He asked me if I was sure.

**Robert**     And you said you were, didn't you?

**Christopher**     Yeah, but I was lying. D'you know what I mean?

*Pause.*

**Robert**     You were *lying*.

**Christopher**   I was lying.

**Robert**   Why?

**Christopher**   Cos I wanted to get out of this place.

**Robert**   Aha! 'The truth will out.' You 'wanted to get out of this place'. You did. It's true.

**Christopher**   But now I don't.

**Robert**   Yes you do.

**Christopher**   No I don't.

**Robert**   I think you do.

**Christopher**   I fucking don't, man.

**Robert**   You do and I'm going to continue to suggest to you that you do whether your conscious mind likes it or not.

*Pause.*

You see, until your *conscious* mind catches up with what your *subconscious* mind wants . . . and *knows*, which is that you, quote, 'want to get out of here', unquote, you're never going to get better. And you're never going to get out of here.

**Christopher**   I'm never . . . ?

**Robert**   Nope. Never. You'll be in hospital – this hospital or some other hospital somewhere – in and out of hospital for the rest of your life.
For the rest of your life.

*Pause.*

**Christopher**   Now I'm scared.

**Robert**   Sure. Of course you are. And I think that that's right. I think if you weren't nervous, you wouldn't be human.

**Christopher**   I didn't say I was nervous.

**Robert**   Well . . . I think you are.

**Christopher**   Oh man. What am I gonna do?

**Robert**   I've just told you what to do.

**Christopher**   Uh?

**Robert**   I just told you what you should do.

**Christopher** *stares into space.*

**Robert**   Chris . . .? The Council . . .? Your housing officer –

**Christopher**   He said I could stay. Doctor Flaherty said –

**Robert**   You know what I think? I think that you think you are scared. And that's all it is, a thought. And I think that it's not your thought.

**Christopher**   What d'you mean?

**Robert**   I think that someone else's thoughts have scared you.

**Christopher**   You think . . . I'm thinking someone else's thoughts?

*Pause.*

Whose thoughts?

**Robert**   I'm saying . . . look . . . Maybe Doctor Flaherty 'projected' his fears of letting you go home on to you and now they're *your* fears.
I'm saying maybe, just maybe Doctor Flaherty . . . unconsciously put his thoughts in your head.

**Christopher**   He put his thoughts in my head. In my head . . . ?

**Robert**   Look, this morning, you were ready to go home. You were so excited. You couldn't wait. You wanted coffee, you had your bags packed, wahey, it was all happening for you. Remember?

**Christopher**   Mm . . .

**Robert**   So what's changed? What's new, my friend? Eh?

*Pause.*

*Nothing.* You had your bags packed.

*Pause.*

Nothing has changed. You're going home. Stop thinking about it. Just do it.

**Christopher**   But, see, the thing is, I got the impression, I got the impression from Doctor Flaherty –

**Robert**   What? Did he say something? What did he say?

**Christopher**   No, but I got the impression –

**Robert**   Well, did you read his mind?

**Christopher** *stares.*

*Silence.*

**Robert**   OK, forget that, bad idea. But but but . . . what I'm saying is How Do You Know? Because really: he *wants* you to go too. He wants rid of you. I should know.

**Christopher**   He wants rid of me?

**Robert**   Yes. He's had enough of you, my friend, we all have, don't jolly well . . . outstay your welcome! N'huh huh huh. Go. Be free.

*Pause.*

N'huh huh huh. D'you see?

*Pause.*

I'm trying to help you.

**Christopher**   I read his mind?

**Robert**   I said to forget that.

**Christopher**   He wants rid of me?

**Robert**   I'm joking. It's a joke!

**Christopher**   The oranges are blue.

*Silence.*

Remember he asked me what colour the orange was?

**Robert**    Mm.

**Christopher**    And I said it was blue. It was. I *saw* that.

*Pause.*

Bright blue. Virtually glowing.

**Robert**    You've had a psychotic episode. Things will be a bit strange for a while. Nothing more insidious.

**Christopher**    'A bit strange'? They were blue.

**Robert**    We will give you medication for that.

**Christopher**    I'm seeing things.

**Robert**    OK OK OK, look. You're not.

**Christopher**    What?

**Robert**    You're not seeing things. I think . . . all right . . . I think you wanted so badly to stay here, subconsciously, that you thought you saw things, or you said you saw things . . .

**Christopher**    You saying I was lying? *Me?*

**Robert**    N . . . I'm saying you were lying. Yes.

**Christopher**    Well, I think *you're* lying.

**Robert**    Because you wanted to stay here. But, you see, if you do stay here, if we give you what we call a Section 3, you will stay here Indefinitely.

**Christopher**    How d'you mean?

**Robert**    We can keep you for up to six months. We can keep you, more or less, for as long as we like.

*Pause.*

**Christopher**    You're prolly not even a proper doctor.

**Robert**   Well . . . n'ha . . . I can assure you, Chris, I am a
'proper doctor'.

**Christopher**   Prove it.

**Robert**   I don't have to prove it.

**Christopher**   Well, that's not fair, is it? What about my
job? D'you know what I mean? I got a job to go to. On a fruit
stall. In the market. I *sell* oranges.

*Pause.*

**Robert**   You sell oranges? (I didn't know that . . .)

**Christopher**   It's true. What am I supposed to tell the
customers? I'm in no condition to sell fruit, d'you know what
I'm saying? Same as I say, I got problems.

*Pause.*

**Robert**   Well. OK. In fact, as I remember, and correct me
if I'm wrong: *First*, Doctor Flaherty *told* you it wasn't orange.
The first thing he said was: 'It's not an orange orange.'
What does that tell you?
You spontaneously made what's called a 'common
association'. You may just have easily said Red.
It's harmless.

**Christopher**   It means something.

**Robert**   What does it mean?

**Christopher**   It's a sign. Cos nobody believes me but I
think it proves it.
He likes oranges. Every day a shipment from Nairobi. I just
*proved* that. I come in here, first thing I see, oranges! They
turn blue. A *signal*.

*Pause.*

**Robert**   OK, look . . . we don't have to concern ourselves
with these things now.

**Christopher**   Yeah, but I'm worried now. I got the fear.

**Robert**   There's nothing to be afraid of.

**Christopher**   You don't know that.

**Robert**   I do, yes, I do. Because. Two reasons. I'll tell you then you'll promise to stop fretting about them, OK? Two things.
One: We can sort these things out when you get home. It's unfair for you to be here while we answer those questions. They are not life-threatening.
They are not a danger to you.
You are not a danger to yourself.
You'll be seeing me once a month and you'll be quite safe and so now I want you to forget all about it.

**Christopher**   Seeing *you*?

**Robert**   If I take over your case, yes. That might happen.

**Christopher**   Why should I see you?

**Robert**   Because it's what I think is best. Because . . . it would be a 'shame' if you didn't.

*Pause.*

**Christopher**   Yeah, but I wanna see Doctor Flaherty.

**Robert**   I'd be better.

**Christopher**   Uh-huh.

*Pause.*

What's the other thing? You said there was two.

**Robert**   The *second* thing is . . .

*Pause.*

Doctor Flaherty . . .
Bruce . . . is somewhat *unorthodox* in his approach. What he's suggesting by keeping you in here is, you have to understand, a little unorthodox. We don't do that any more if we can help it. We want you out there.
We want you to go *home*. D'you see?

**Christopher**   Yeah, but he's worried, that's all.

**Robert**   I know, and that's because, you see, Bruce, Bruce, see, Bruce is a little, as we say in the trade, He's a Tee-Pee and a Wig-Wam.

*Pause.*

He's Too Tense.

*Pause.*

Heh heh. No I'm kidding. But he is . . . you know, he's just a, you know, *I'm* the Head of Department. I'm the Boss. I'm the Big Cheese.

*Pause.*

The Top Banana.

*Pause.*

OK, this is very delicate. It's not something we know an awful lot about. But it's my specific field of research, I'm writing a book on it as a matter of fact.

**Christopher**   You're writing a book? Really? You're really writing a book?

**Robert**   Well . . . I blush to the toes of my shoes to admit but . . .

**Christopher**   What's it about?

**Robert**   Well . . . it's about . . . it's about psychosis diagnosis. In . . . people like you.

**Christopher**   People like me, yeah?

**Robert**   You see, I believe there may be a cognitive therapy which we can substitute for the drug palliatives normally associated with psychosis.
My 'assertion' is this:
There is a Cultural Specificity to the apparently delusionary nature of some of your beliefs.
There are Antecedents for some of the beliefs you hold.

'Cultural Specificity and Cultural Antecedent or
Schizophrenia'.
You see? '*Or* Schizophrenia'. Not 'And'. That's what it's
called.

*Pause.*

**Christopher**    What does Doctor Flaherty think about it?

**Robert**    Well . . . uh . . . he hasn't read it yet.

**Christopher**    I meant about me seeing you.

**Robert**    Oh well . . . OK . . . well, the thing is . . . see . . .

*Pause.*

Doctor Flaherty isn't in possession of the full facts.

**Christopher**    Why not?

**Robert**    Because he's not an authority. I'm an authority.
He isn't.

*Pause.*

Because there are things you do and things you believe which
he, within his culture, can only recognise as Insanity.

*Pause.*

Which I personally believe, for what it's worth, is rather
narrow-minded . . . it's what some people call 'Culturally
Oppressive'.

**Christopher**    Insanity.

**Robert**    It means he has a tendency to overlook, in our
discussions at any rate, your cultural identity.

*Pause.*

It's nothing . . . it's no big deal . . . it's an oversight, that's all. It's
a vastly complex subject. People get things wrong.

**Christopher**    What did he say?

**Robert**   OK, look. I don't want you to take this the wrong way because I don't think he meant it in a pejorative sense . . . I'm quite sure . . . but it indicates a gap in his knowledge which I'm trying to *redress*.

**Christopher**   What did he say?

**Robert**   Well . . . well . . . since you asked . . . I think he has a very real fear that . . . our response to you is weighted by our response to your colour. I personally feel that *should* be the case; it *should* be a factor in your treatment and that we shouldn't overlook such a thing. Otherwise what happens, in institutions such as this, there develops what's termed 'ethnocentricity'; which ordinarily is fairly harmless but in certain instances is not far off . . . well . . . it is the progenitor of 'cultural oppression', which in turn leads to what we call 'institutionalised racism'.

**Christopher**   Racism?

**Robert**   Yes. And the danger is that in a sense you maybe end up, in a sense, being 'punished' for the colour of your skin. (*Beat.*) For your ethnicity and your attendant cultural beliefs. (*Beat.*) You are sectioned and locked up when you shouldn't be. (*Beat.*) Because you're 'black'.

*Silence.*

**Christopher**   I'm being *punished*?

**Robert**   Maybe that's too strong a term but but but –

**Christopher**   Because I'm *black*?

**Robert**   Well, you see, the system is *flawed*. People of ethnic minority are not well catered for, it's a well-known fact. I've just expressed it clumsily –

**Christopher**   He said that? I'm locked up because I'm black?

**Christopher** *stands abruptly.*

**Robert**   No, that's not what was said. Let me finish –

**Christopher**    Where is he?

**Robert**    OK, calm down.

**Christopher**    The fuck does that mean?

**Robert**    Chris Chris Chris Chris –

**Christopher**    He really said that? It's cos I'm black?

**Christopher** *heads for the door and* **Robert** *rushes around and blocks his way, trying to hold him back.*

**Robert** (*struggling with him*)    Look, listen, look, listen, look, listen, look, listen, look, listen . . .

*Pause.*

Chris, my dear dear fellow, just sit down and listen for one moment please.
Our colonial antecedents are latent and barely suppressed –

**Christopher**    What shit!

*He paces angrily.*

**Robert**    This really is a storm in a teacup.

**Christopher**    Punished by who?

**Robert**    Chris, please, sit down. Sit down. Come on now. I implore you.

**Christopher** *sits and thinks, stares, quiet.*

**Christopher**    Who am I being punished by?

**Robert**    Well, by, by, by the *system*. The system tends to punish without meaning to.

**Christopher**    That's why I see things? I'm being punished?

**Robert**    No . . . Chris –

**Christopher**    That's why I hear things? These *mental . . . fucking* . . . the noises I hear . . . the *fear* –

**Robert**    What he said was –

**Christopher**    You said I'm not thinking my own thoughts –

**Robert**    No –

**Christopher**    Well, whose thoughts am I thinking?

**Robert**    Nobody –

**Christopher**    Doctor Flaherty's . . . ?

**Robert**    OK, let's not get off the track –

**Christopher**    He smokes too much *drugs*, man, d'you know what I mean? He likes his puff. I can tell.

*Silence.*

**Robert**    Sorry . . . you said? About . . . dr . . . ?

**Christopher**    He *told* me I should go back out there and *score* some puff, man. Why did he say that? Because I'm black?

**Robert**    O . . . K . . . but . . . I'm sure . . .

*Pause.*

'Puff'. For *him* . . . ? Or . . . for . . . ?

**Christopher**    He goes he goes he goes, If I was only in here to get drugs I'd come to the wrong place. He said the drugs out there, right, were more *fun*.

**Robert**    I see, well . . . I see . . . well. (*Beat.*) When was this?

**Christopher**    Earlier. Before you got here.

**Robert**    Just before or . . . some time before?

**Christopher**    Just before. This morning.

**Robert**    Oh.

*Pause.*

What else did he say?

**Christopher**    He said it was 'voodoo'. That's why I'm here. Voodoo. Remember?

**Robert**    W . . . ell . . .

**Christopher**    And he lied to me. He said he was letting me out when he was just gonna keep me in here longer just like you said, man. He lied to me.

*Pause.*

And and and he keeps looking at me funny.

*Pause.*

Can I have a cup of coffee now?

*Blackout.*

# Act Three

*Next afternoon.* **Bruce** *and* **Christopher** *sit facing each other; the bowl of oranges is on the table between them.*

**Bruce** *has a report in front of him and is reading from it.*

**Christopher** *is smoking a cigarette and staring into space.*

**Bruce**  'He ordered the patient to peel the orange . . .' I didn't *order* you.

*He reads.*

'. . . establishing that it was the same under the skin. That the flesh was the same colour as the skin.'
OK, I *suggested*, Chris, I *prompted*, and maybe I shouldn't have but, you know, it's not as if this was the first time, was it? You don't need my help to start . . . (*reading*) seeing things . . .

*He reads.*

*Pause.*

Do you really believe this? Do you really think I . . . what? I'm . . . 'Provocative, unorthodox, patronising . . .'? And . . . 'Possibly *on drugs* . . .'? I mean, this is . . . this just . . . I've never heard anything so ridiculous in my life!

*He reads.*

'He snatched away a cup of coffee given to the patient by the consultant . . . He used the pejorative epithet "nigger".'

*Silence.*

I did not, um, my God, I didn't use the epithet . . . nnn . . .

*He stares.*

I did not call you a . . . um, um, um, a . . . I didn't say that.

**Christopher**  Say what?

**Bruce**    Would you please put that out? Christopher? The cigarette.

**Christopher** *mashes out the cigarette on the table.*

**Bruce**    I, I, I, didn't call you a, a, a, um, a . . . a . . . (*beat*) 'nigger'.

**Christopher**    You said 'uppity nigga'. You did. Deny.

**Bruce**    Only because *you* did. My God! It was a quote!

**Christopher**    Yeah, but you shouldn'ta said it.

**Bruce**    Oh, so so so only you can say it?

**Christopher**    It's not polite.

**Bruce**    I know it isn't and, um . . .
I'm sorry, excuse me . . .
I feel sick . . .

*He steadies himself.*

*Pause.*

Do, do you really think I meant it? Do you really think I meant to 'provoke' you? I was giving vent to 'racist' proclivities?

**Christopher**    Look. I don't know. I don't know. I just want to go home.

**Bruce**    What is wrong with you?
Are you out of your mind?
Have you been drinking?

**Robert** *appears in the doorway, listening.*
*He enters and sits down.*

**Robert**    You asked to see me.

**Bruce**    We have a meeting.

*Pause.*

We agreed to meet today. The three of us. Unless you know of something that could have happened to change that.

**Robert**    I'm on the Authority, Doctor Flaherty, of course I know.

*Pause.*

There was a Management Hearing this morning.

**Bruce**    Yes I know. How convenient.

**Robert** *shrugs.*

**Bruce**    So. Where do we go from here?

**Robert**    Well, you know, actually, what I think is that you and I need to be alone together.

**Bruce**    OK. Uh. Christopher, would you mind coming back in . . . ?

*He checks his watch.*

**Christopher**    But I've just packed.

**Bruce**    That's all right. Just go back to your ward and I'll send for you.

**Christopher**    But I've just –

**Bruce**    Please, Chris.

**Christopher**    But we –

**Bruce**    Please?

**Christopher**    But . . . I'm getting out today. My twenty-eight –

**Bruce**    OK, look –

**Christopher**    My twenty-eight –

**Bruce**    Chris –

**Christopher**    My twenty –

**Bruce**    I know but –

**Christopher**    My –

**Bruce**    All right!

*Pause.*

Not now. *Later.* I'll send for you.

**Christopher**    I already packed.

**Bruce**    I know.

**Christopher** *stands and exits.*

**Robert**    I know exactly what you're thinking and before you say anything I want you to know it was nothing to do with me. (*Beat.*) I mean, whatever he said to the *rest* of the Authority . . . (*Beat.*) I had no idea that he'd done this when I went into that Management Hearing this morning. I knew he wanted to make a complaint to the Authority – I tried to talk him out of it. That's the last I knew of it.

**Bruce**    But you 'are the Authority'.

**Robert**    OK . . . I'm a *representative* at *Management Hearings.* One of many.

**Bruce**    But yesterday you said you 'are the Authority'.

**Robert**    Only sometimes . . . sometimes it's me, yes, who . . . whoever is . . . *everybody* runs it. It's a different person each week depending on . . . it's more of a *committee* than a, than a . . .

**Bruce**    The point is . . . have you read this?

*Pause.*

**Robert**    Of course I've read it.

**Bruce**    Don't tell me. You've read it because: you wrote it?

**Robert**    Of course I didn't write it. What kind of bastard do you take me for?

*Pause.*

**Bruce** (*reading*)   'After some initial difficulty following the patient's interpretation of events, the Authority reached a consensus that if the said orange was indeed to be viewed as blue for the purposes of the analogy . . .' For the purposes of . . . ?

*He gives* **Robert** *a look.*

**Bruce**   '. . . then clearly as a blue-skinned orange it was indeed in the minority given that other citruses are ordinarily orange, yellow or . . .'

*He gives* **Robert** *a look.*

**Bruce**   'By asking the patient to peel the "minority" orange . . . and declaring the insides of the orange to be of equally unusual colouring, the house officer seems to have implied . . .'
What did you *say* to him?

**Robert**   I didn't say anything.

**Bruce** *reads.*

**Bruce**   'The Authority reached a consensus.' How?
Did everybody think of the the the stupidest things they could think of and then put them all in a hat?
By playing a drinking game?
Small children wouldn't come up with this.
*Monkeys* could do better using *sign language.*
For God's sake!

**Robert**   'Monkeys'.

**Bruce**   Yes.

**Robert**   Is that another analogy?

**Bruce** *stares.*

**Robert**   It's too easy to misinterpret, Bruce. You really have to be more careful.

**Bruce**   Well. Do you agree with 'the Authority'?

**Robert**    I rather think I should remain impartial on this
one. Besides, they're more interested in your side of the story.
Give me a statement and they'll probably leave you alone.

**Bruce**    Give you a 'statement'. But I haven't done anything!
I can't . . . believe . . . has it really gone that far? Can't you
. . . can't I just talk to them?

**Robert**    Well . . . not really. There's a Procedure.

*Pause.*

**Bruce** *reads.*

**Bruce**    'The Authority recommends that a senior
consultant confers treatment with an outpatient programme.'

**Robert**    I think it's a good idea.

**Bruce**    Why?

**Robert**    I'm a senior consultant. He already knows me.

**Bruce**    What do you get out of it?

**Robert**    I don't 'get' anything. It's just expediency.

**Bruce**    'Expediency'. The Path of Least Resistance.

**Robert**    Absolutely.

**Bruce**    OK. So. You want to take over the case. And . . .

*Pause.*

Then you can continue Your Research?

*Pause.*

And Then You Can Finish Your Book. Is it a good book? It
must be, you'll go to any lengths to finish it . . .

**Robert**    You're on very thin ice here, Flaherty.

**Bruce**    'The Search for the Holy Grail'.
What a chapter heading that would make.
'A Cure for Black Psychosis'.
Imagine. No more bed crises. No more hospitals.

We'd save a bundle on Care in the Community.
You'd become Professor overnight.

**Robert**   I *beg* your pardon!

**Bruce**   You heard.

**Robert**   Are you out of your mind?

**Bruce**   You'll be the toast of Academia the World Over.
Imagine! A golden opportunity to distinguish yourself from all
the other boffins; To be the Eggiest Egg Head of them all; to
be *different* from all the other odious little careerists on the
gravy train kissing management arse. To be Up There with
all the other Cambridge wonderboys in their bow ties and
tweed, flapping about the 'corridors of power' with their
pricks in each other's pockets. What's wrong with just *doing
your job*?

*Pause.*

**Robert**   It's the Maudsley actually.

**Bruce**   I'm sorry?

**Robert**   I read Psychiatry at the Institute of Psychiatry at
the Maudsley Hospital in Dulwich. Not Cambridge.

**Bruce**   Oh, the Maudsley, big difference.

**Robert**   I really recommend you go there. I think you need
to go there. And I don't mean for training.

*Pause.*

You're already the subject of an inquiry. If the Authority asks
for a Psychiatric Report I'll be in a very awkward position.

*Silence.*

**Bruce**   OK. OK. Look . . . have you never heard . . . listen,
uh, Doctor . . . did you hear Christopher refer to himself,
somewhat effacingly, somewhat ironically as a, quote, 'uppity
nigger'? Did you hear him say that?

**Robert**   It was unmistakable.

**Bruce**    And presumably you heard me quoting him, also, I offer, somewhat ironically?

**Robert**    I'd steer clear of irony if I were you. You're not Lenny Bruce.

**Bruce**    It was . . . it was a *nuance*. It was . . . the way I said it . . . with a note of familiarity . . . because I know him . . . and –

**Robert**    It's not for me to characterise your 'nuances', Doctor. And if you ask me, yes, perhaps it was somewhat 'provocative and unorthodox'.

**Bruce**    Only to you.

**Robert**    How do you mean?

**Bruce**    It was provocative and unorthodox to you because, well, frankly, it would be, wouldn't it? Perhaps you don't get out enough.

**Robert**    You're doing it again: you're being provocative.

*Pause.*

I'm sorry, Doctor. It's pejorative whichever way you say it and these days racial epithets just don't wash.

**Bruce**    'These days'. I see. Did they use to?

*Pause.*

**Robert**    You know what I mean.

**Bruce** *seizes the report and tears it into bits.*

**Robert**    May I . . . ?

*He produces a mobile phone and dials.*

This is Doctor Robert Smith, can somebody send Christopher over here immediately please . . . upstairs . . . yes . . . no, I'm in the consultation room with Doctor Flaherty . . . no, he's my . . . no, he was but . . . he . . . n . . . I understand but . . . well he's my patient now.

*He puts the phone away.*

**Bruce**    What did you tell him?

**Robert**    Bruce –

**Bruce**    What have you done?

**Robert**    It's his complaint; why don't you ask him?

**Bruce**    I intend to. (Just as soon as you've slithered off.)

**Robert**    Actually, that's not possible, I'm afraid. Not until I've briefed the patient.

**Bruce**    . . . What?

**Robert**    That's the procedure. I can't allow you to be alone with him. It's a question of Seniority as much as anything else. Perhaps if you'd shown some respect for Seniority in the first place; if you'd listened to Somebody Who Knew, we wouldn't be in this mess.

**Bruce**    So I'm not allowed to see Chris any more without you being present?

**Robert**    Anything you want to ask you must ask the Authority.

**Bruce**    I just *asked* 'the Authority' and I think 'the Authority' is *lying*.

**Robert**    I'm presenting you with the opportunity to defend yourself. That's the Procedure. What more do you want?

**Bruce**    Christ, it's so transparent.

**Robert**    Oh, do stop whining, Bruce. Before somebody nails you to a cross.

*Pause.*

Oh. While I'm here I should mention that I've been keeping a diary.

**Bruce**    A *diary*?

**Robert**   A diary of my research, but there are things in it which might be relevant to your case.

*He produces a diary from his jacket pocket.*

Now you've stopped blustering I should read you some things before my patient returns.

**Bruce**   You just happened to have it on you.

**Robert** (*reading*)   'Twenty-sixth of October: Mention Antecedent Programme to Doctor Flaherty and he laughs. Not interested in providing African-Caribbean and African patients for research purposes.'

**Bruce**   I didn't laugh . . . I . . . this is silly . . .

**Robert**   Which suggests you have been obstructive towards me from the off. I'm your *supervisor*. You don't turn down a request like that unless you have a very good reason.

**Bruce**   I . . . look . . . I have professional reservations . . . ethical reservations about –

**Robert**   About what?

**Bruce**   About using patients as, as guinea pigs in, in, in –

**Robert**   'Guinea pigs'? Honestly, Bruce. 'Monkeys, guinea pigs, voodoo . . .' You've an entire menagerie of piccaninny slurs to unleash.

**Bruce**   *What?*

**Robert**   Can you not see how this could be *interpreted* – by the Authority, for example? You have to admit it doesn't look good.

**Bruce**   Then don't show it to the Authority.

**Robert**   I beg your pardon.

**Bruce**   I said, don't . . . show . . . Doctor Smith . . . please . . . it's . . . it's . . . do we have to show them this?

**Robert**   We'll pretend you didn't say that, shall we?

*Silence.*

**Bruce** *just stares.*

**Robert** *flips over a few pages.*

**Robert**    'Twenty-fourth of October: Flaherty implies research funds being used to keep me in, quote, "dickie bows and putters".'

**Bruce**    We were *drunk*. After the rugby.

**Robert**    *You* were drunk.

**Bruce**    And and and you *agreed* with me. It was a joke!

**Robert**    You invite me to watch the rugby with you and then you insult me. You drag me home for a chunk of rancid cheese on toast, get pissy-drunk on Bulgarian hock and start haranguing me about iniquity in the medical profession like some kind of mildly retarded student activist, then you expect the Nobel Peace Prize for Services to Psychiatry.
Why are you so threatened by my ideas?

**Bruce**    Because . . .

*Pause.*

Because they're *shit*, Doctor.
The research is banal and it's all been done before *anyway*. It's Old News. It's *R. D. Laing* in a gorilla suit.
It isn't empirical.
And it isn't a PhD.
It isn't a Book.
A *cookbook* would be more ground-breaking.
It's a waste of resources and money and everybody's time and you know it.

**Robert**    What are you implying?

*Pause.*

You see, this is just the type of verbiage –

**Bruce**    Verbiage?

**Robert**    Which people find so highly offensive about you, Bruce. This is how you wind up under investigation.

**Christopher** *walks in carrying a large holdall and sits down.*

**Christopher**    Hope I'm not interrupting.

**Robert**    Hello again, Christopher. I'm so sorry to send you away like that. We've concluded our meeting now and as soon as the doctor has asked you one or two more questions you'll be on your way.

**Christopher**    I'm going home now?

**Robert**    You're going home.

**Christopher**    Oh boy. Oh man. I'm going home.

**Bruce**    Chris, have I upset you in any way?

**Robert**    You can't ask that question.

**Bruce**    Why – because he might answer it?

**Robert**    Jurisprudence dictates.

**Bruce**    Are there 'charges pending'?

**Robert**    You are Under Investigation, yes. If there are charges to be answered then you will be suspended pending the inquiry.

**Bruce**    What charges?

**Robert**    Negligence.

**Bruce**    'Negligence'?

**Robert**    Racial harassment.

**Bruce**    What else? I'm intrigued.

**Robert**    Abuse.

**Bruce**    'Abuse'. Well. I was waiting for that. 'Abuse'. Mm. You know what I think? I think people abuse the term 'abuse'.

**Robert**    Excuse us a moment please, Christopher.

*He takes* **Bruce** *by the elbow and marches him to a far corner of the room.*

**Robert**   Doctor Flaherty, if Christopher stays in here indefinitely under a Section 3 and is diagnosed with paranoid schizophrenia, the rest of his life will be ruined.

**Bruce**   He won't get the help he needs without that diagnosis.

**Robert**   It would be negligent.

**Bruce**   Please, Doctor Smith, yours is an *arbitrary diagnosis*. You've observed him in one interview. It's my word against yours.

**Robert**   Two interviews.

**Bruce**   And you saw something entirely different to what I've seen.

**Robert**   That's the ICD 10 for you. Observation and interview.

**Bruce**   I think . . . look, I think he's suicidal.

**Robert**   He's not suicidal. He's just depressed.

**Bruce**   He's depressed because he's schizophrenic.

**Robert**   He's depressed because he's *here*. Exactly how old is Christopher?

**Bruce**   Twenty-four.

**Robert**   Twenty-four. And how do you think it feels for Christopher – a bright, fun, charismatic young man – to be locked up with chronic, dysfunctional mental patients twice his age?
People with a history of institutionalised behaviour.
People who harm themselves.
People with drug problems, who are suicidally depressed, who scream and laugh and cry routinely for no apparent reason – when they're not *catatonic*.

Have you thought about how intimidating and frightening
that must be for him? Night after night after night, with no
let-up.
Have you thought about what that does to a young man?
It's Like Going to Prison.
It's *cruel*.

*Silence.*

Now.
I have examined the patient in depth.
I have consulted with a social worker and a CPN.

**Bruce**   When?

**Robert**   In this morning's Management Hearing.
And we believe this patient will receive the treatment he
needs in the community.
We concur that the community is the right and proper place
for him.
We believe that we would be failing him by keeping him.

**Bruce**   So . . . it's all been settled then. I'm being overruled.

**Robert**   To say the fucking least, Doctor.

**Bruce**   So why have an inquiry.

**Robert**   Well, you see, for what it's worth, we're beginning
to wonder whether this patient should ever have been
sectioned in the first place.

**Bruce**   The, the, the police sectioned him with a 136.

**Robert**   Well perhaps they were being 'ethnocentric'.
He was drinking.
He was depressed.
The hospitals are full of men like Christopher.
The prisons are full of men like Christopher.
Ordinary men whose lives have flown apart and they've
found themselves in a market one day 'acting funny'. Next
day they've been locked up and a week later they're on the

coast of a crack-up. Don't you think it's time we did
something about it?

*Pause.*

Look at him! He's a mess. Well? What have you got to say for
yourself?

*Pause.*

(*To* **Christopher**.) I'm sorry, Chris.

**Christopher**    No, you just talk amongst yourselves. D'you
know what I mean?

**Bruce** *stares into space.*

*Silence.*

**Bruce**    You're not going to show me any support here, are
you? As my supervisor? As a mentor? A friend?

**Robert**    That would be highly inappropriate.

**Bruce**    You've made up your mind. You support this
allegation.

**Robert**    Not the allegation, just the inquiry. I'm afraid so.

**Bruce**    Golly. Just wait till I tell my wife.

*Pause.*

Maybe *you'd* like to tell her. Next time we invite you for
dinner. Next time she slaves over a hot stove to put food in
your mouth.

**Robert**    I'd hardly call Welsh rarebit 'slavery'.

**Bruce**    Next time I buy you a ticket for the rugby.

**Robert**    If you'd let me buy them we'd have sat in the
members' stand.

**Bruce**    I don't even *like* fucking rugby. Bunch of hairy twats
running about biting each other's ears off.

*Pause.*

**Robert**    Bruce, I'm simply asking you to give me a statement. Give the Authority your side of the story. Now. Have you got a lawyer?

**Bruce**    Why should *I* get a lawyer? *You* get a lawyer. *Prove* this. I can't believe this is even happening!

**Robert**    I really don't understand why you're taking it so personally. Why are you so angry?

**Bruce**    Because it *is* personal. You're somebody I trusted. I confided in. I thought you were on my side. I thought you and me could make a difference. Which is why I invited you over. My wife cooked. Nourished you. I should have choked you.

**Robert**    Bruce. You wanted me for your supervisor. Your mentor. You expect me to recommend your consultancy one day.

**Bruce**    And why did you agree – if not to get research material out of me? To finish your book. To . . . to . . . Doctor Sm . . . please . . . I don't know why . . .

**Robert**    I agreed because I liked you.
I thought you had promise.
I thought, such is my vanity, that you could learn something from me. Is that so difficult to believe?
Are you really so insecure?

*Silence.*

*They stare at each other.*

**Christopher**    You got any jelly babies?

**Bruce** (*to* **Christopher**)    Did I upset you yesterday? When I asked you to peel that orange?

**Bruce** *tosses* **Christopher** *an orange from the bowl and he catches it.*

**Robert**    I really don't think this is a good idea.

**Bruce**    Did that upset you?

**Christopher** *looks at* **Robert**.

**Bruce**    No, don't look at him, look at me.

**Christopher**    D'you know what I mean? I'm thirsty. I
need a Coke.

**Bruce**    You'll get a Coke if you answer my question.

**Robert**    Doctor Flaherty.

**Bruce**    Did that upset you when you peeled the orange?

**Christopher**    No.

**Bruce**    Later, when you got to thinking about it, were you
upset?

**Christopher**    No. It interested me.

**Robert**    You're pushing your luck, Flaherty.

**Bruce**    'No'? Oh, OK. Why do you think I asked you to
peel the orange?

**Christopher**    To see what colour it was inside.

**Bruce**    And what colour was it? In your own words.
Without any help from me.

**Christopher**    In my own words. Blue.

**Bruce**    Peel another one. See if it's still blue.

**Robert**    I really don't recommend this.

**Bruce**    Go ahead, Christopher. Why not? I'll even let you
eat it.

*Pause.*

**Christopher** *peels the orange.*

*Pause.*

*He begins eating it suspiciously.*

**Bruce**    What colour is the orange, Chris?

**Christopher**    Blue.

**Bruce**    OK. And what do you think that means?

*Pause.*

**Christopher**    Something to do with my dad.

**Robert**    OK, that's enough.

**Bruce**    Something to do with your dad? OK.

**Robert**    I said –

**Bruce**    And what do you think I think it means?

**Robert**    Enough!

**Bruce**    What do *I* think it *represents*?

**Christopher**    S . . . omething to do with my dad?

**Robert**    This is not the time or the –

**Bruce**    Any idea what?

**Robert**    . . . Place.

**Christopher**    Nope. No idea, man.

**Bruce**    Well, I have no idea either.

**Christopher**    Maybe it's a signal.

**Robert**    . . . I must insist –

**Bruce**    Or a coincidence?

**Christopher**    No, it ain't a coincidence.

**Bruce**    What's it a signal of then?

**Christopher** *produces the crumpled newspaper cutting from his pocket and smooths it out, shows it to* **Bruce** *who shakes his head slowly.*

**Christopher**    Idi Amin Dada. See? '*Da-da.*' That's another signal.

**Bruce**    No, Chris . . . I'm sorry . . . please.

*He touches* **Christopher** *on the arm.*

**Bruce**    Put it away now. Concentrate.

**Robert**    Don't you think you're being a bit arbitrary?

**Bruce**    What?

**Robert**    Why should he put it away?

**Bruce**    'Why'?

**Robert**    Yes. He's not a child. Why should he?

*Pause.*

**Bruce**    Because he cut it out of the newspaper.

**Robert**    'Because he cu –' Really?

*Pause.*

And and and what makes you think that?

**Robert** *snatches the article from* **Christopher** *and examines it.*

**Bruce**    It's just a hunch.

**Robert**    Well, my hunch is that he didn't. My hunch is that his mother gave it to him. What is it about this particular disclosure that makes you so uncomfortable, Bruce?

**Bruce**    What makes me uncomfortable is that this morning he told me his father was Muhammad Ali. He'd seen him on breakfast television winning Sports Personality of the Century.

*Silence.*

**Robert** (*to* **Christopher**)    Is this true?

**Christopher**    1974. *Zaire. Think* about it, man.

**Robert** (*to* **Bruce**)    Why didn't you tell me this before?

**Bruce**    Before when?

**Robert**    Before . . . *now.*

*Pause.*

You told me about his mother in Feltham, blue oranges and the Chevrolet but the Rumble in the Sodding Jungle you didn't deem appropriate! Jesus wept!

*Silence.*

OK. Now. OK, what have we got here? One of the most feared men in history and one of the most loved. Both immensely powerful. Both role models. Both of African origins.

**Christopher**    Both Muslim Fundamentalists.

**Bruce**    Abso-fucking-lutely! Christopher, please. I want you to concentrate on the orange –

**Robert**    I am warning you, Doctor –

**Bruce**    What does it represent now?

**Robert**    It was stipulated at the Management Hearing that you have no further contact –

**Bruce**    What do you think Doctor Smith thinks it represents?

**Robert**    Listen . . . Christopher –

**Christopher**    That's easy –

**Robert**    Chris . . . ? Bruce –

**Bruce** (*to* **Robert**)    Grant me this one favour, please: listen to your patient. Chris?

**Christopher**    He says it's a *person.*

**Robert**    I never –

**Bruce**    A person. What kind of person?

**Robert**    – said anything of the –

**Christopher**    A Brother.

**Robert**    No. That's enough.

**Bruce**   And do you agree with that?

**Christopher**   I don't know.

**Robert**   What I said was . . . what I meant was . . . and you obviously completely misunderstood me . . . was –

**Christopher**   You did –

**Robert**   Enough! Let me finish –

**Christopher**   You said it was *me*.

**Robert**   OK, OK, OK, OK, OK, OK, OK . . . OK . . . Now . . . I commented, I merely *commented* that . . . I *suggested* that it was an unfortunate demonstration which could potentially be viewed . . . by *somebody* very vulnerable . . . by a patient . . . as an 'analogy'.

**Bruce**   But it wasn't an analogy.

**Robert**   All right . . . nevertheless . . . it could be 'taken the wrong way'. It could 'cause offence' . . .

**Bruce**   But it didn't cause offence –

**Robert**   Well . . . in hindsight –

**Bruce**   In whose hindsight?

**Robert**   OK, all right, whatever the *fucking semantics*, it was an unfortunate incident –

**Bruce**   It wasn't an incident –

**Robert**   All right, it was very, very . . . it was *upsetting*. He was upset by it, that's all and so, so, so I brought it up in the Management Hearing –

**Bruce**   Oh, *you* brought it up in the Management Hearing?

**Robert**   What?

**Bruce**   You said *you* brought it up. You just said that. You said you brought it up at the Management Hearing this morning.

*Silence.*

**Christopher**    And he said I should learn to lick my own balls. He did. Ridiculous but true.

*They all stare at each other.*

**Robert** *rubs his eyes.*

**Christopher**    (Do I look like a contortionist?)

**Bruce**    So . . . Doctor . . . *you* made the Complaint. *You* lodged this complaint with the Authority.

**Robert**    The patient was very upset. He was in no state to –

**Bruce**    Were you upset, Christopher?

**Christopher**    What? When?

**Robert**    He was. Take my word for it.

**Bruce** (*to* **Christopher**)    Are you upset now?

**Robert**    I'm going to go berserk in a minute. I am trying to straighten this out for you! I am trying to help.

*He takes out his packet of cigarettes shakily.*

(*Lighting up.*) Give you the benefit of my . . . erudition . . . and experience . . . as a Senior . . . as Senior . . . *Senior* Consultant . . . *Head* of Department . . .

**Christopher** *takes a cigarette and the lighter and lights it, also shakily.*

**Bruce**    Christopher, if I upset you, I apologise. Sincerely. I didn't mean to upset you. Did I say anything else that upset you?

*Pause.*

Chris?

**Christopher**    You put thoughts in my head.

**Bruce**    What kind of thoughts?

**Christopher**    Just thoughts.

**Robert**    I have to insist this stops right now.

**Bruce**    Shut up. Chris . . . ?

**Robert**    Christopher. Not another word.

**Bruce**    Can you think of anything specific?

**Christopher** *stares at* **Bruce**.
**Christopher** *spits the orange out and stares at the remaining segments in his hand.*

**Christopher**    The thoughts I have are not my thoughts. He said that I think your thoughts.

**Bruce**    *Doctor Smith* said?

**Christopher**    And that's why I have to get out of here.

**Robert**    That's not what I said.

**Christopher**    I've gotta get outta here cos of you, man!

**Robert**    Look . . .

**Christopher**    Cos you're *bad*.

**Robert**    OK . . . Christopher –

**Christopher**    And now I don't, I don't, I don't know what to think! I don't know what to think any more.
When I do think, it's not my thoughts, it's not my voice when I talk. You tell me who I am.
Who I'm not. I don't know who I am any more!
I don't know who I am!

**Robert**    Chris –

**Bruce**    Chris –

**Robert**    It's being here that's doing this to you. This place –

**Bruce**    You're still very confused –

**Robert**    You can't think straight in this place. How can you . . . ?

**Bruce**   You're safe here, OK? It's quiet –

**Robert**   Apart from the bloodcurdling screams of all the other mental patients –

**Bruce**   Chris, you need to do this, you must try and stay a little longer –

**Robert**   You can leave now if you want to leave now –

**Bruce**   Chris –

**Robert**   But you have to want to.

**Christopher**   I do want to!

**Bruce**   Are you sure you're ready?

**Christopher**   No, man, I'm not sure of anything!

**Robert**   Christopher –

**Bruce**   Chris –

**Robert**   Listen . . . list –

**Bruce**   Chris –

**Robert**   Chris –

**Christopher**   OK OK OK JUST SHUT UP JUST SHUT THE FUCK UP FOR ONE MOMENT FOR GOD'S SAKE YOU ARE DRIVING ME AROUND THE BEND!

*Silence.*

**Bruce**   OK, look . . . (*To* **Robert**.) Could we have a minute alone please?

**Robert**   Absolutely not.

**Bruce**   I don't think you're in a position to argue any more.

**Robert**   You're only making it worse.

**Bruce**   Nevertheless. I think you should.

**Robert**   OK! OK! It's *your funeral.*

**Robert** *exits.*

*Silence.*

**Christopher**    What the fuck do you want, Bruce?

**Bruce**    Well, um, well, um, I'd like you to understand that this is a very serious situation.

**Christopher**    Yeah, but the thing is, like he said, I don't think you should take it so personally, d'you know what I mean?

*Pause.*

**Bruce**    Well. You know. Um. I know. Yes. I'm trying.

**Christopher**    When somebody does something you don't like, you should just learn to laugh. D'you understand?

**Bruce**    Y – OK – OK. The thing is, Chris . . . see . . . I'm not very good at this. I'm not very good at . . . Not Taking Things Personally.
That's all. I like to . . . Get to the Bottom of Things.

**Christopher**    You don't say.

**Bruce**    No, I'm not being funny. Things here at the hospital, at work, I take personally sometimes. I'm ever-mindful of the way one's *professional* life impacts upon one *personally*. Just as what happens to *you* here impacts upon your personal, private life. It's all related. So you see, when you took your complaint to the Authority one of the things they concluded was that I had been 'unprofessional'. Which is in their jurisdiction to decide – they are generally more venerable – more experienced, judicious beings than I. However, the upshot is that depending on what happens now . . . I could possibly be sacked in the *first month* of my training! It isn't your fault. And I am not taking that personally. But what I would like to point out to you is that, that could well affect *both* our personal, private lives in a, in a *terrible, disastrous* way. OK? Do you understand now?

**Christopher**    Don't patronise me.

*He eyeballs* **Bruce**.

*Pause.*

**Christopher**    I had a life before this. I had a job. On a stall in the market.

**Bruce**    That's what I'm saying.

**Christopher**    I got stuff to go back to. I've got my mum.

**Bruce**    Your mum can't help you just now.

**Christopher**    She needs me. She gets lonely. I miss her.

*Pause.*

**Bruce** (*gently*)    Chris . . . you don't know where she is, do you?

*Pause.*

You see, my point is, when they let you out this afternoon, the theory is that you'll go back to your family. To your community. But you don't have any family, do you? Not any more. Not so far as we know. And, the thing is, should you come back, should you ever need to return and ask for my help, I might not be here.

**Christopher**    I'll see Doctor Smith.

**Bruce**    I . . . I know. But, um . . . you can see him *anyway*.

**Christopher**    How d'you mean?

**Bruce**    There's no need for you to press ahead with this complaint. If you no longer want me to treat you, I won't.

**Christopher**    I don't.

**Bruce**    Then I won't. Fine.

**Christopher**    Cos you put your thoughts in my head.

**Bruce**    OK, well . . . you know, Chris, I really didn't mean to. Maybe other people have put thoughts in your head too but they're not going to be birched for it. Do you, do you, do you see what I mean?

**Christopher**    No.

**Bruce**    I'm saying . . . look . . . I don't know what Doctor Smith said to you yesterday evening, OK, I have no idea – actually, I have a pretty good idea and I think . . . I'll be honest with you. I think Doctor Smith 'coached' you in what you had to say to the Authority.

*Pause.*

I think he put words in your mouth.

**Christopher**    He put words in my *mouth*?

**Bruce**    Yes. Not literally. Figuratively. OK . . . don't get excited.

**Christopher**    No, *you* put words in my mouth. When I said I wanted to stay and I was scared, that was you. That's why I'm here now! Cos of *you*!

**Bruce**    No. OK? Now . . . no. Just . . . No. Just let me read you something.

*He takes a pamphlet from* **Christopher**'s file.

I'm going to give you this to take with you. Whether you stay or go. This is what the World Health Organisation has to say about schizophrenia. I don't want to alarm you, but I want to explain to you what you've just said. I want to 'demystify'.

*He reads.*

'The most intimate thoughts . . . are often felt to be known or shared by others and explanatory delusions may develop, to the effect that natural or supernatural forces are at work to influence the individual's thoughts and actions in ways that are often bizarre.'
Sound familiar?

*Long pause.*

**Christopher** *snatches the pamphlet, screws it up, throws it on the floor.*

**Christopher**    You're just trying to get off the hook now.

**Bruce**    Just listen to me. You don't know what you're talking about.

**Christopher**    Why? Cos I'm an 'uppity nigga'?

**Bruce**    Look. Shut up a minute.

**Christopher**    Oh, that's very nice, that's lovely. It's all coming out now.

**Bruce** *slams his fist on the table.*

**Bruce**    This isn't a game! My career is on the line!

**Christopher**    Your 'career'?

**Bruce**    And your . . . your . . . you have got so much to *lose*! We both have, don't you see this?

**Christopher** *kisses his teeth.*

**Bruce**    Chris . . . please, for God's sake. Can you remember what you did in the market with the orange? Can you see how that could get you into a lot of trouble? If you were doing that . . . on the estate, for example, I don't know what could happen . . .

**Christopher**    I never trusted you. Mm-mm. I liked you, but I never trusted you.

**Bruce**    What . . . ?

**Christopher**    You told me I could have a Coke, yeah? In front of a witness you said I could have a Coke if I answered your questions and I answered your questions so where is it? D'you think I'm thick or something?
D'you think I'm thick?
You told me you were letting me out and now you're not. What's going on, Bruce?

**Bruce**    I am, Christopher, I will.

**Christopher**   When?

**Bruce**   Soon.

**Christopher**   Oh 'soon'.

**Bruce**   When you've been diagnosed properly. You must try and be patient.

**Christopher**   I don't *believe* you. You call me nigga. You say it's voodoo.

**Bruce**   It was a joke!

**Christopher**   Oh funny joke. Do you see me laughing?
I've got one for you. I'm gonna Lay Charges.
Cos I ain't staying here, man.
You'll never keep me locked up, white man. This is one nigga you don't get to keep, white man. Cos I'm gonna bark every time you come near. D'you understand?

**Bruce**   Is this you or is it . . . someone else? Is this the *illness* or is it . . .

*Pause.*

Maybe you're just *like* this.
Maybe you're just . . . A Wanker.
I mean . . . why do you say these things?

**Christopher**   Cos you ruined my life!
Cos you're Evil.
And you're a Fascist.

**Bruce**   How dare you!

**Bruce** *stands.*

**Christopher** *stands.*

**Bruce**   You fucking idiot . . . What Have You *Done*?

**Christopher** *starts to laugh.*

**Bruce**   What's funny? Stop laughing! Shut up! You stupid fucker. What are you laughing at?

**Robert** *is standing in the doorway, unseen.*

**Bruce**    Shut up! For fuck's sake!

**Christopher**    The look on your face, boy!

**Bruce**    You won't be laughing when you get home. You won't be laughing when you start losing your marbles all over again and hearing voices and jabbering like a lunatic and shitting yourself because you think your fucking zombie neighbours are coming to eat your brains, you mad bastard! You *idiot*!

**Christopher**    'Love Thy Neighbour' it says. How can I love my neighbour when my neighbour is fascist?

**Bruce**    They're black! All your neighbours are. It's a *black neighbourhood*. You you you *moron*. You stupid *fool*. Are you *retarded*? Jesus! This is the thanks I get for *rotting* in this stinking hellhole, pushing shit uphill, watching what I say, tiptoeing around, treading on eggshells, *kissing arse* while you sit around laughing and squawking and barking like a freak. You didn't know if you were Arthur or Martha when you came in here and this is the thanks I get. Now you're upset. *Now* I've upset you. Good. *Good.* See how much you like it.

*He sees **Robert** standing in the doorway and stares.*

**Robert**    When you use the term 'neighbour', do you mean it rhetorically or 'generically'?

*He comes into the room, takes an orange from the bowl, sits and peels it as he talks.*

Because it's just occurred to me that when Chris talks about his 'neighbour', he might not mean literally 'the people next door'. Do you, Chris? Nor would you mean 'sibling' should you allude to a 'Brother'. (*Eating.*) Neighbours is Everybody, isn't it? People in the street giving you a wide berth. Women on escalators holding their handbags that little bit tighter as you pass. People looking straight through you as if you're not even there. Football hooligans. Skinheads. Throwing bananas. Your workmates. Bruce and I can only *guess* at the horror of suffering from acute paranoia *and* being one of a culturally oppressed minority. What a combination.

*Pause.*

And we ask each other, Why are our mental hospitals full of young men like this? Why do you *think*?

*Pause.*

**Bruce**   Robert-Robert-Robert-Robert-Robert-Robert-Robert . . .

*Pause.*

Doctor . . .

**Robert** *produces a prescription pad from his pocket and writes a prescription.*

**Robert**   Why don't you report to outpatients and they'll organise you a car.

*Pause.*

Chris? Then you can go home.

**Christopher**   Do you think I should?

**Robert**   Yes. You must.

**Christopher**   Do you think I'm ready? Really?

**Robert**   Yes. You're ready. You can't stay in here for ever. (*To* **Bruce**.) Can he?

**Bruce**   I . . . what . . . ?

**Robert**   Do you want to get better?

**Christopher**   Yeah . . . I want to.

**Robert**   Then you must do what you must do. Be brave.

**Christopher**   Uh?

**Robert**   Be brave.

**Christopher**   'Be brave'?

**Robert**   Yes. Because you are brave. You're a very brave young man and you've done really well. This is your prescription.

*He hands* **Christopher** *the prescription.*

**Christopher**   Did you hear what he said?

**Bruce**   I'm sorry. I didn't mean it.

**Christopher**   Why d'you say those things, man?

**Bruce**   I really am sorry.

**Christopher**   My God. It really is a game of two halves with you, d'you know what I mean?

**Bruce**   Are you all right?

**Christopher**   What? *No.* That *hurt*, man. I can't stay in here if you're gonna say shit like that. D'you know what I mean? Running your mouth. It's *rude*.

**Bruce**   I know.

**Christopher**   It's *weird*.

**Bruce**   Sure.

**Christopher**   How would you like it?

**Bruce**   I know . . . I'm sorry.

**Christopher**   No, you don't know. How would you like it?

**Robert**   If you'd like to make another complaint –

**Christopher**   I *am* complaining. I'm complaining to *him* and he's not even listening.

**Bruce**   I . . . I think I need to sit down.

**Robert**   Would you like to lodge a complaint with the Authority?

**Christopher**   No. I'm OK.

**Robert**   It's really no trouble.

**Christopher**    I'm all right now.

**Bruce** *sits.*
*He stares.*
*They regard him as he picks up a piece of orange peel, examines it, bites into it.*

**Robert**    I'll get one of the nurses to book your first outpatient appointment.

**Christopher**    Thanks.

**Robert**    Don't mention it.

**Christopher**    No really, safe, man. I appreciate it.

**Robert**    It was the least I could do.

**Christopher**    Thank you.

**Robert** *offers his hand and they shake hands.*
**Bruce** *just stares from one to the other.*
**Christopher** *goes to* **Bruce**, *suddenly staring oddly.*

*Silence.* **Christopher** *picks up an orange.*

**Christopher**    Have you ever stuck your dick in one of these?

**Bruce** *looks at him a little nervously.*

**Christopher**    One time I tried it with a grapefruit. At Christmas. It's OK but it chafes a bit. The juice stings. On the ward I seen one boy do it with bugs. Straight up. Puts a bug on the end of his willy. A cockroach. Just on the tip. He likes the way it wiggles. You think there's bugs in this?

**Bruce**    I'm . . . sorry . . . ?

**Christopher**    Is there bugs in this?

**Bruce**    Chris . . . please . . .

**Christopher**    I need a girlfriend, man. D'you know what I mean? That's all I ever wanted. I just wanted somebody nice to be with. A lady.

*Silence.*

**Robert**    Take it with you if you like.

**Christopher**    Uh?

**Robert**    Take it. Be my guest.

*Pause.*

It's a gift. It's time to go home.

**Christopher**    What have you done to it?
What have you put in it?
What are you staring at?

**Christopher** *ignores the orange.*
*He stares from* **Robert** *to* **Bruce** *suspiciously.*
*He moves a few steps towards the door, then stops.*

**Robert**    That's right. Off you go. Go home and listen to
some reggae music.

**Christopher** *stares at* **Robert** *for some time.*
**Robert** *eventually smiles and indicates the door.*
**Christopher** *goes.*
**Robert** *looks at* **Bruce***, shakes his head, 'tuts' at length.*

**Bruce**    'Reggae music'?

**Robert**    What is it in Africa, 'jungle'? N'ha ha ha. (*Snorts.*)

**Bruce** *picks up an orange.*

**Bruce**    Well. That's that, then.

**Robert**    How do you mean 'That's that'?

**Bruce**    I've fucked it up, haven't I?

**Robert**    Oh, I see what you mean. Well . . . yes.

**Bruce**    I'll never make Consultant.

**Robert**    You still want to?

**Bruce**    Well . . . of course . . . but . . .

**Robert**   Oh.

*Long silence.*

**Bruce**   Unless . . .

**Robert**   What's that?

**Bruce**   We . . . don't really have to pursue this . . . now . . .
do we?.

**Robert**   Well, I can tell you, I'm in no hurry to have the
good name of my department dragged through the mud.
Thank you very much.

**Bruce**   No . . .

*Pause.*

Not to mention . . . not to mention your Professorship.

**Robert**   My Professorship? How does it affect that?

**Bruce**   Well . . . it doesn't.

*He retrieves and carefully unfurls the remains of the screwed-up, torn
report.*

So . . . where do we go from here?

*Pause.*

I mean . . . what's the procedure? We were getting on quite
well. Until . . . this . . . disagreement.

**Robert**   It's a little more than that.

**Bruce**   But it's . . . I mean . . . uh . . . you're a good
supervisor.
And a valuable mentor.

*Pause.*

I'm pr . . . I'm privileged. I'm grateful to you.

*Pause.*

For . . . putting me straight.

*Pause.*

One could have made a dreadful mistake.

*Pause.*

Perhaps . . . I could . . . buy you a drink . . . to express my
gratitude.
Debrief.
I could read your manuscript.

*Pause.*

**Robert**    No. I don't think we'll do that.

**Bruce**    W . . . why not?

**Robert**    Well. The thing is . . . I'll tell you something.

*He takes the report from* **Bruce** *and smoothes it out.*

**Robert**    I don't like you, Bruce.
You talk too much.
You get in the way.

*Silence.*

You see, sick people come to me.
All creeds and colours.
They are suffering.
They go away again and they no longer suffer.
Because of me.
All because of me.
And there's nothing wrong with that.
Is there?

**Bruce**    Who do you think you are? God?

**Robert**    How does Archbishop of Canterbury sound? N'ha
ha ha.
You will not be employed by this Authority again. We made
a mistake. It's a little Darwinian, I admit, nevertheless.
Goodbye.

*He hands* **Bruce** *the orange.*

You can eat it on the train.

**Bruce** *stares at the orange in his hand.*
*He slumps in his chair.*
*He peels the orange.*
*He stares at* **Robert**.
**Robert** *goes.*

**Bruce**    I want to make a complaint.

**Robert** *stops.*

**Bruce**    I'd like to lodge a complaint with the Authority.

**Robert**    Sorry?

**Bruce**    I'm ready to give you a statement.
What's the procedure for that?

**Bruce** *bites into the orange. They stare at each other.*

*Blackout.*

# Notes

7   *Snakebite*: A pint made with equal quantities of cider and
    beer. Many pubs in the UK refuse to serve snakebite
    because people anecdotally get intoxicated more quickly
    than when drinking either cider or beer alone.

8   *Sorted for es and whiz*: This phrase is the title of a 1995
    song by the British band Pulp (it's on the album *Different
    Class*). Es and whiz are the 'popular' clubbing drugs
    ecstasy and speed. According to the band's singer, Jarvis
    Cocker, a friend described hearing drug dealers at
    Glastonbury using the phrase.

9   *Where's the Tamazie Party?*: Temazepam is one of the
    benzodiazepine class of drugs, which are psychoactive.
    It is sometimes used for the short-term relief of
    insomnia, but has also been widely misused. In the UK,
    Temazepam is a class C drug.

9   *smack*: heroin.

12  *Radio Rental*: Rhyming slang for 'mental'.

12  *schizophrenic*: Schizophrenia is a disease of the brain
    which is currently thought to affect one in a hundred
    adults. It does *not* mean 'split/multiple personality' (this
    condition, now known as a dissociative identity disorder,
    is very rare). Schizophrenia is characterised by a range
    of symptoms and these can have a huge impact on an
    individual's ability to think and function well. The
    symptoms of schizophrenia can be subdivided into three
    types: positive, negative and cognitive. Positive symptoms
    include delusions (thinking or believing things which are
    demonstrably untrue/unlikely, which can't be explained
    culturally, and which are resistant to logic or reasoning)
    and hallucinations (hearing or seeing things which aren't
    there). Positive symptoms, in particular, tend to come
    and go: people with schizophrenia don't tend to be

delusional all the time. Negative symptoms include
a lack of motivation, reduction in quantity and quality
of speech, increasing withdrawal from both people and
activity, and a lack (or inappropriate expression) of
emotion, often called 'flat affect'. Cognitive symptoms
include impairments in memory, learning, concentration
and decision-making. (The boundary between cognitive
and negative symptoms is, in everyday life, blurred and
impossible to define accurately.) There is much about
schizophrenia which is not fully understood, including
its causes (though there seem to be a range of risk
factors which are both genetic and environmental), the
reasons for the dopamine-affecting antipsychotics'
effectiveness in managing the positive symptoms of the
illness, and, indeed, whether the different types of
schizophrenia (paranoid, disorganised, catatonic,
undifferentiated) are one disorder manifesting in
different ways or whether what we currently call
schizophrenia is actually more than one disorder with
some overlapping symptoms.

13   *Borderline Personality Disorder*: A mental illness which is
characterised by instability in moods, interpersonal
relationships, self-image and behaviour. BPD has a set
of symptoms which are identifiable, but the effects and
intensity of these symptoms vary significantly from
person to person. Symptoms of BPD include: sensation
seeking (impulsivity), self-harm, extreme emotion/mood
swings, explosiveness, fear of abandonment, unclear/
unstable self-concept, emptiness, difficulties in
maintaining meaningful relationships, dissociation.
Like schizophrenia, the causes of BPD are still not
fully understood. However, recent studies suggest a
combination of genetic influences with challenging
development events are usually present (most people
with BPD report difficult or traumatic childhoods).

14   *Welsh rarebit*: As Robert later says, this is (slightly
glorified) cheese on toast.

14   *The Frog*: Slang for the French.

15   *Warning warning warning! Alien life form approaching, Will*
     *Robinson*: A line (or, almost a line) from the science-
     fiction TV show *Lost in Space*, which ran for three
     seasons and was first aired between 1965 and 1968.
     This is one of the robot's lines – another one which is
     well known is the phrase 'Does not compute'.

19   *Because I'm a Brother?*: Here, 'Brother' is colloquial for
     'black'. This is the first explicit indication that we get of
     the role that race, racism and cultural difference will
     play in *Blue/Orange*.

19   *Zebedee*: The jack-in-the-box character from the
     children's animated TV show, *The Magic Roundabout* (the
     English version of which was first broadcast between
     1965 and 1977) who did, indeed, bounce around a lot.

20   *'Yardie'*: In the UK, this tends to refer to a member of a
     Jamaican (or West Indian) criminal gang (usually
     dealing in drugs such as crack cocaine). The word
     appeared in this usage during the 1980s. It is also used
     by Jamaicans about fellow Jamaicans – the word was a
     slang name for those living in the 'government yards' of
     Trenchtown, West Kingston, Jamaica.

21   *Sesame Street*: US children's TV show which was first
     broadcast in 1969 and is still running today. It is an
     educational programme which is well known for its use
     of Jim Henderson's Muppets, and which deals with real
     and current issues (including the attacks on the Twin
     Towers on 9/11). In relation to Christopher's comment,
     it's worth noting not only that *Sesame Street* employed an
     ethnically diverse cast from the start, but also that it was
     occasionally considered controversial for doing so.

22   *My twenty-eight days*: This is the length of time that a
     Section 2 (see below) assessment order lasts.

23   *Section 2*: Under the 1983 Mental Health Act, Section 2
     is an assessment order. It lasts up to twenty-eight days,
     and it cannot be renewed: this is why Bruce and Robert
     are arguing about what to do for (or with) Christopher
     now that his assessment time is ending. Under Section
     2, a person can be detained in hospital, despite their
     refusal, if two doctors and an Approved Mental Health

Professional agree they are suffering from a mental disorder to such a degree that s/he ought to be in hospital (for his/her own health, or for the safety of the person or the protection of others). Further, treatment (such as medication or ECT) can be given against the person's wishes.

23   *Section 3*: Under the Mental Health Act 1983, Section 3 is a treatment order. Initially, it can last up to six months, and it can be renewed. It is instituted in the same way as Section 2 (that is, following assessment by two doctors and an Approved Mental Health Professional). However, for a Section 3 treatment order, the doctors need to be clear about the diagnosis and proposed treatment. Further, they need to be confident that 'appropriate medical treatment' is available for the patient (hence this being a treatment order rather than an assessment order).

23   *Level Ones*: Patients in the UK are classified according to their care needs. Level 0 means that care can be met on a normal ward; Level 1 means the patient is at risk of their condition deteriorating, or has a higher level of care whose needs can be met with advice and support from a critical care team. Robert is suggesting that Christopher's need for a bed is not sufficiently high.

23   *Wacky Races*: A US animated television series featuring twelve cars racing against each other as the drivers compete to be the 'World's Wackiest Racer'.

24   *Specialist Registrar Training*: In the old system of medical career progression, this was advanced training in a specialised area of medicine; once completed a doctor became a consultant. This phase came after five or six years of medical school and a minimum of three years' further training, and the specialist training took four to six years. In the new system, introduced in the UK from 2005, the process altered slightly: the equivalent phase now is known as the Specialty Registrar.

25   *the White City Estate*: White City is an area of west London (in the Borough of Hammersmith and Fulham). The White City Estate was built in the 1930s as part of

the slum clearance programme. It is a large estate, and a
2009 report found that it was one of the most deprived
areas of London. This report also noted that it has a
much higher than average proportion of black or black
British residents. (Though it does not break this group
down further, Bruce's claim that the estate is a
predominantly Jamaican community, though perhaps
somewhat overstated, is likely to be accurate.)

25   *Peripatetic childhood*: Peripatetic means travelling from
place to place – so a peripatetic childhood is one which
is itinerant, rather than settled in long-term locations.
It is often associated with disrupted schooling.

27   *ICD 10 Classification*: The 10th revision of the
International Statistical Classification of Diseases and
Related Health Problems. It is a medical classification
list by the World Health Organisation (WHO), and is
the standard diagnostic tool for epidemiology, health
management and clinical purposes (including the
analysis of the general health situation of population
groups and to monitor the incidence and prevalence of
diseases and health problems). The 10th revision was
endorsed in 1990 and came into use in 1994. Currently,
twenty-five countries (WHO member states) use the
ICD 10. Mental and behavioural disorders are in
Chapter V. Work for the 11th revision is scheduled to
be completed in 2015.

27   *Linus blanket*: A security/comfort blanket (Linus is a
character from the cartoon strip *Peanuts* who is rarely
seen without his blue blanket).

28   *It's a movable feast*: Literally, a holy feast day which isn't
attached to a particular date (such as Easter and the
feast days connected with it). Here, though, Robert is
using the phrase metaphorically, suggesting that
diagnoses to do with mental health shift in response to
context and circumstance.

28   *semantics*: The relationship between words and things,
and between language, thought and behaviour: that is,
how behaviour or outcomes is influenced by words.
Semantics as a branch of linguistics is particularly

interested in changes in meanings. Here, Robert is saying that he and Bruce are disagreeing over the meanings of words, and is arguing that his use of language and, in particular, medical definitions and terminology, is more persuasive than Bruce's.

28    *prognosis*: A doctor's prediction of the likely outcome of an illness.

29    *Shepherd's Bush*: An area of west London, in the Borough of Hammersmith.

30    *Community psychiatric nurse* (CPN): A fully trained psychiatric nurse who sees patients in the community, rather than in hospital (often the person's own home, but sometimes in clinics such as a GP's surgery). CPNs liaise with the patient and both primary and secondary care services.

31    *Lancet*: Founded in 1823, *The Lancet* is published weekly and is one of the best known and respected of medical journals (in 2012, it was ranked second out of 153 among general medical journals). Proofreading for it, Robert implies, is a limited role (rather than, say, writing for it). *Welsh Doctor Weekly* doesn't exist, but acts as a stand-in for something rather unlike the *Lancet* – small scale, not widely read or regarded.

31    *OTT*: Over the top.

33    *R. D. Laing*: British psychiatrist and writer (1927–89), and one of the most influential figures in the anti-psychiatry movement (though Laing himself avoided this term). His key works include *The Divided Self* and *The Politics of Experience*. Laing aimed to alter the way that madness is perceived by humanising psychosis. He was particularly concerned – and Robert echoes him here – with the seductive myth of 'normality'. Laing's personal problems – including clinical depression and alcoholism – led to him being prevented from practising medicine in Britain in 1987. Bruce's attitude to Laing is now shared by many (and his views on the use of antipsychotics are now considered – particularly with the development of second-generation antipsychotics – out of date and incorrect). However, it is worth noting that the anti-

psychiatry movement has had a lasting and important
impact, particularly in relation to the viewing of patients
as individuals, and an increased understanding of the
role of upbringing, culture and society as well as
biological processes – and that normality might be as
nebulous a concept as madness.

33  *Allen Ginsberg*: American poet (1926–97) who is known as
one of the leading writers of the Beat generation. He is
perhaps best known for his epic poem *Howl* (1956),
which opens with the lines 'I saw the best minds of my
generation destroyed by / madness, starving hysterical
naked . . . ' In this poem, and much of his other work,
Ginsberg rails against materialism, conformity and
capitalism. During the 1960s he was active in the anti-
Vietnam War movement; he was also open about both
his homosexuality and his communist sympathies.
Bruce's incredulity at Christopher quoting Ginsberg in
this conversation probably relates to Ginsberg's reputation
as a prolific drug user, particularly of LSD, which has
hallucinogenic properties: in the context of a psychiatric
unit where much effort goes into controlling and
managing psychosis, Ginsberg is likely to raise eyebrows.

34  *Government guidelines*: Robert is most likely referring to the
Department of Health, which has responsibility for
government policy in relation to health and social care
in England. (Most, although not all, health policy for
Scotland, Northern Ireland and Wales is now devolved
to their governments – though this was not the case
when *Blue/Orange* was written.) Robert is talking about
the move – discussed in the commentary – to care in the
community, which had begun to happen in the post-war
period, but was hastened by the closing of mental
institutions and asylums from the mid-1970s, and (most
relevantly here) by the interventions of the Conservative
government under Thatcher in the 1980s.

34  *Institutionalised*: Usually associated with either patients or
prisoners who have become dependent after a (typically
long) period in an institution. This affects their ability to
reintegrate and function in the 'outside' world.

35    *Haloperidol*: One of the first-generation antipsychotics.
      These drugs, though relatively effective in controlling
      the positive symptoms of schizophrenia (delusions and
      hallucinations), often have unpleasant side effects,
      including tremors, abnormal movements, muscle stiffness
      and restlessness. First-generation antipsychotics have
      been available since the 1950s, and their development
      revolutionised the care of patients as, before this,
      therapeutic options were very limited. However, initial
      enthusiasm for them was tempered by a realisation of
      their significant side effects.

35    *Hanger Lane Gyratory*: A large, complex roundabout
      system in west London.

41    *Idi Amin* (mid-1920s–2003): Amin was the military
      dictator and President of Uganda from 1971 to 1979.
      Having risen through the ranks of the Ugandan army,
      he seized power in a military coup. His dictatorship was
      brutal: international observers and human rights groups
      estimate that between 100,000 and 500,000 people were
      killed during his rule, which was characterised by an
      escalation in human rights abuses, ethnic persecution and
      extrajudicial killings, as well as economic mismanagement,
      nepotism and corruption. Amin was polygamous,
      marrying at least five women (he divorced three of
      them), and fathering a large number of children (sources
      vary on the question of how many). After the Uganda–
      Tanzania War, Amin fled to exile in Libya and then
      Saudi Arabia.

42    *'The Butcher of the Bush'*: Amin was often referred to as
      'The Butcher' for the reasons outlined above.

43    *Haringey*: An area of north London.

44    *'Le Monde est Bleu comme une Orange'*: Robert slightly
      misquotes the opening line (one of the most famous
      surrealist phrases) of a poem by Paul Éluard. The poem
      actually begins, 'La terre est bleue comme une orange'
      (The earth is blue like an orange).

44    *Paul Éluard* (1895–1952): This is the nom de plume of
      Eugène Grindel, French poet and one of the founding
      members of the Surrealist movement (see previous note).

45   *There's a Tintin book. Tintin and the Blue Oranges*: Created
by the Belgian artist Georges Remi (1907–83), writing
under the pen name Hergé, *The Adventures of Tintin* is one
of the most successful and loved series of comics ever.
There are twenty-four books in the series, published in a
wide range of languages from the 1930s onwards (the
final one posthumously). The series – in particular its
early titles – has been critiqued for perpetuating a range
of racial and ethnic stereotypes. *Tintin and the Blue Oranges*
is not a book, but a film (released in 1964 and based on
an original script by André Barret). It was the second
live action Tintin film to be released, and the plot
revolves around a new invention – a blue orange which
can be grown in the desert and solve world famines. A
book of the film was published. It was not a traditional
Hergé Tintin book, rather a book with conventional
text and photos based on the film.

45   *Tintin was banned in the Belgian Congo. They thought he was a
communist*: As Bruce says, Robert is 'making this up' – or
perhaps misrecalling information. One of Hergé's early
works, *Tintin in the Congo*, first written in 1931, suffered
from Remi's early prejudices and racism; it depicts the
Congolese in stereotypical and paternalistic ways. He
later redrew several pages because they were so
imperialist. Complaints are still raised about this book
in particular, and it was not published in English until
1995, with the colour version not appearing until 2005.
In 2012 Belgian courts dismissed a case brought to ban
the book. Robert's suggestion that Hergé was thought a
communist is also dubious: his early works portray
Bolsheviks in an extremely negative light and the
Belgian paper he wrote for during the Second World
War became a propaganda paper for the Nazis. This is
a good example of Robert sounding much more
convincing than he actually is.

49   *Ethnocentric*: Judging other people or cultures according
to one's own (particularly in relation to language,
religion, culture, traditions and beliefs), characterised
by the belief that one's own culture is superior. It often

leads to false assumptions being made, and in mental
health diagnoses, when health professionals have to
make decisions about whether a person's thinking is
disordered or delusional, these can become – as Robert
is suggesting here – entangled with issues around
cultural difference.

52   *Prozac*: The best-known trade name of the drug
Fluoxetine, an anti-depressant first introduced in the
mid-1970s. Due to its wide appeal and use, Prozac is
probably one of the medications most frequently
mentioned in popular culture.

52   *Viagra*: The best-known trade name of a drug used to
treat erectile dysfunction.

55   *The Ivy*: Reputedly one of the most celebrity-packed
restaurants in London. Located near Covent Garden,
it opened in 1917.

55   *La Rochelle*: Beautiful harbour city in western France.

63   *QPR*: Queens Park Rangers Football Club, which is
based in White City (since the mid-1960s, in the Loftus
Road stadium).

72   *'Common association'*: A word frequently associated with
another word (e.g. cat and dog).

72   *Nairobi*: Capital of Kenya.

76   *Institutionalised racism*: As discussed in the Commentary,
the Macpherson Inquiry (1998) into the death of Stephen
Lawrence in 1993 brought the idea of institutional
racism into the public realm in the UK. The report
found the Metropolitan Police to be riddled with
institutional racism, defining this as 'the collective
failure of an organisation to provide an appropriate and
professional service to people because of their colour,
culture, or ethnic origin'. But the term has been around
since the Black Power movement of the 1960s, and can
apply to any system, organisation or institution which
demonstrates prejudice against people on the grounds
of their race. Suman Fernando's *Cultural Diversity, Mental
Health and Psychiatry* (2003), looks at the ways in which
the mental health system has been permeated by racism.

77    *the system. The system tends to punish without meaning to*:
      Robert is here attempting to explain how institutional
      racism continues to function (that is, inequalities and
      prejudices have become built into it).

87    *Lenny Bruce* (1925–66): American comedian and satirist
      whose performances were outspoken, politically charged
      and controversial for their time. Bruce was frequently
      arrested and charged for obscenity, and has gone down
      in history as a comedian who blazed a path for a frank,
      uncensored style of comedy.

89    *piccaninny slurs*: Racial caricatures and jibes.

90    *Empirical*: Based on verifiable evidence, achieved though
      observation and experiment, usually in medicine/science.
      Bruce is therefore challenging the very basis of Robert's
      research and methodology.

90    *verbiage*: Wordiness; profusion of words – and the
      implication is often that there is either little content, or
      that the content is obscure. We might, then, read
      Bruce's exclamation in response to this as partly to do
      with the fact that Robert, more than Bruce, might be
      best accused of verbiage.

92    *catatonic*: Catatonia is an abnormality of movement and
      behaviour, and is associated with a range of other
      mental illnesses. It can involve repetitive/purposeless
      over-activity or an extreme loss of motor skills.
      Catatonia has become less common in recent decades
      and so Robert may well be using the word in its more
      colloquial sense, to mean lethargic and unresponsive.

93    *The police sectioned him with a 136*: Section 136 is part of
      the 1983 Mental Health Act. It is an order that applies
      to a person found in a public place who the police
      consider to be mentally disordered, and allows a police
      officer to take that person to a 'place of safety' (usually
      either a police station or a hospital). Once at this place,
      the person subject to a Section 136 police officers' order
      is further assessed and, in some cases, either a Section 2
      assessment order or a Section 3 treatment order is
      implemented. Here, Bruce is effectively explaining to

Robert the barest outlines of why and how Christopher
was sectioned.

98   *Muhammad Ali*: Born 1942 (original name Cassius Clay),
Ali was an American heavyweight boxer, civil rights
campaigner and activist. He is widely regarded as one
of the greatest boxers of all time – if not *the* greatest. He
changed his name when he converted to Islam in 1964,
and had to take several years out of his boxing career
since he was stripped of his licence and titles as a result
of his refusal to fight in the Vietnam War. Eventually
his case was upheld (he argued that he would not serve
on religious grounds) and he returned to boxing,
becoming the only boxer to win the heavyweight
championship three times in a row. In the mid-1980s,
Ali was diagnosed with Parkinson's disease (an illness
which is common in those who have suffered head
traumas). He remains one of the most iconic sportsmen
of all time, famous, not only for his fighting but also for
his personality, his humanitarian work, and his place in
the history of black civil rights, and of political and
religious freedom. He is the subject of a number of films
and documentaries.

98   *1974. Zaire*: One of the most famous fights in the history
of professional boxing, known as the 'Rumble in the
Jungle.' The fight – between Ali and then-champion
George Foreman – took place in Kinshasa, Zaire, on
30 October 1974. Foreman was the favourite, but Ali
won the fight and regained his title.

106   *World Health Organisation*: As their website says, the
World Health Organisation (WHO) is 'the directing
and coordinating authority for health within the United
Nations system. It is responsible for providing leadership
on global health matters, shaping the health research
agenda, setting norms and standards, articulating
evidence-based policy options, providing technical
support to countries and monitoring and assessing
health trends.' Set up in 1948, its constitution states that
its objective 'is the attainment by all people of the
highest possible level of health'.

111   *a game of two halves*: A cliché from football commentary used to describe games where there is a big difference between play in the first and second halves. The phrase is often used in other contexts as well to indicate that someone's luck has turned. Here, though, Christopher is pointing to the abrupt shift in Bruce's tone and attitude towards him.

111   *Running your mouth*: Talking without thinking; usually associated, as here, with loudness, speed and hurtfulness.

113   *Reggae music*: Reggae music was initially developed in Jamaica in the 1960s. Of course, as we know, Christopher is not from Jamaica. Jungle music, which was popular in the mid-1990s, is also Jamaican and Caribbean-influenced, rather than African. Robert is being considerably more generalised in his assumptions about race than Bruce ever was.

# Questions for Further Study

1.  Penhall describes *Blue/Orange* as 'a very political play, and a play about spin'. What do you think he means by this?
2.  Robert says: 'Schizophrenia is the worst pariah. One of the last great taboos. People don't understand it. They don't want to understand it' (p. 52). To what extent does *Blue/Orange* seek to change or challenge this statement? How does it do this? Is it successful?
3.  Analyse the power dynamics of *Blue/Orange*: how do the characters' relationships develop, and what does this tell us about them?
4.  'All of my plays are about the impulse towards freedom [ . . . ] But they are also about the dangers of escape and liberation' (Penhall in Aragaray *et al.*, p. 78). How does Penhall negotiate this territory in *Blue/Orange*?
5.  Do your opinions and feelings about the characters develop or change during the course of the play? How does Penhall's use of dialogue and structure affect this?
6.  How does Penhall's use of language, repetition and imagery affect the meaning of the play? What is distinctive about his writing style?
7.  What does this play say about political correctness? How does it say it?
8.  Discuss the significance of the setting of the play. How might you try to realise this in performance? How have previous productions approached this?
9.  At several points in the play, Christopher is silent while on stage. What do you think happens in these moments? What is the effect of his silence on the shape and meaning of the play? How might the actor's performance affect these moments?
10. Is Robert a figure of the establishment or of the counter-culture? What is the importance of the tension between the two?

11. Compare and contrast the play's representation of mental illness with another work (for example, Sarah Kane's *4.48 Psychosis* or Anthony Neilson's *The Wonderful World of Dissocia*). How do these representations differ in their approach, meaning and effect?

12. How does this play intervene into, or contribute towards, discussions about institutional racism in the post-Macpherson Inquiry era?

13. Why do you think Christopher fixates on Idi Amin and Muhammad Ali? What does this tell you about his character? What does it – or anything else in the play – say about masculinity, or a possible crisis of masculinity?

14. What do you think the place of humour is within this play? How does Penhall use jokes, and why?

15. As an actor, how would you portray any one of the characters in *Blue/Orange*, and how would you prepare for the role? How might you use your physicality and voice, your body language, and the space of the theatre at specific and key points in the play?

16. How effective is the three-act, dialectical play structure? Why do you think it is used? Does it have any limitations?

17. *Blue/Orange* is set in the UK, and bound up with the structures of the NHS. Does it speak more broadly, to other places or institutions and, if so, how?

18. William C. Boles argues that, 'While the play opens up a dialogue about the institutionalisation of racism in treating black patients, Penhall's ultimate message is that the hubris of doctors in terms of their treatment of patients is an even more problematic danger facing the profession' (*The Argumentative Theatre of Joe Penhall*, p. 133). How far do you agree with this statement? Is it the play's 'ultimate message'?

19. What do you think are the particular challenges of staging *Blue/Orange*? How would you approach these as a director, an actor, or a designer?

20. What does this play tell you about structures of a) care or b) power? What arguments does it stage about these, what questions does Penhall ask about them, and how does the play address or answer these questions?

RACHEL CLEMENTS is a lecturer in Drama, Theatre and Performance at the University of Manchester. Her research focuses on contemporary theatre practice and, in particular, British playwriting and dramaturgy, and the relationships between performance and politics.